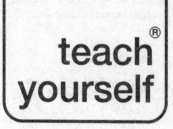

teach yourself®

sikhism

The *Teach Yourself World Faiths* series aims to present all the essential information required by the reader who has no previous knowledge of the religion, but who wants to feel confident in dealing with members of the faith community – both in terms of their beliefs and attitudes, and also the practical details of their culture, ceremonies, diet and moral views.

Titles include:

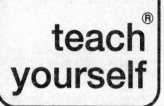

teach
yourself

sikhism
w. owen cole

For over 60 years, more than
40 million people have learnt over
750 subjects the **teach yourself**
way, with impressive results.

be where you want to be
with **teach yourself**

For UK order enquiries: please contact Bookpoint Ltd, 130 Milton Park, Abingdon, Oxon OX14 4SB. Telephone: +44 (0) 1235 827720. Fax: +44 (0) 1235 400454. Lines are open 09.00–18.00, Monday to Saturday, with a 24-hour message answering service. Details about our titles and how to order are available at www.teachyourself.co.uk

For USA order enquiries: please contact McGraw-Hill Customer Services, PO Box 545, Blacklick, OH 43004-0545, USA. Telephone: 1-800-722-4726. Fax: 1-614-755-5645.

For Canada order enquiries: please contact McGraw-Hill Ryerson Ltd, 300 Water St, Whitby, Ontario L1N 9B6, Canada. Telephone: 905 430 5000. Fax: 905 430 5020.

Long renowned as the authoritative source for self-guided learning – with more than 40 million copies sold worldwide – the **teach yourself** series includes over 300 titles in the fields of languages, crafts, hobbies, business, computing and education.

British Library Cataloguing in Publication Data: a catalogue record for this title is available from the British Library.

Library of Congress Catalog Card Number: on file.

First published in UK 1994 by Hodder Education, 338 Euston Road, London, NW1 3BH.

First published in US 1994 by Contemporary Books, a Division of the McGraw-Hill Companies, 1 Prudential Plaza, 130 East Randolph Street, Chicago, IL 60601 USA.

This edition published 2003.

The **teach yourself** name is a registered trade mark of Hodder Headline.

Copyright © 1994, 2003 W Owen Cole

Typeset by SX Composing DTP, Rayleigh, Essex

Printed in Great Britain for Hodder Education, a division of Hodder Headline, 338 Euston Road, London NW1 3BH, by Cox & Wyman Ltd, Reading, Berkshire.

Hodder Headline's policy is to use papers that are natural, renewable and recyclable products and made from wood grown in sustainable forests. The logging and manufacturing processes are expected to conform to the environmental regulations of the country of origin.

Impression number   10 9 8 7 6 5 4

Year   2010 2009 2008 2007 2006 2005

acknowledgements

First I must acknowledge the help that I have received from my brother Piara Singh Sambhi who introduced me to Sikhism and nurtured me in it. Secondly, his wife Avtar and son Jaswant continue to answer my many questions and improve my knowledge and appreciation of their religion. Professor Bakhshish Singh has kindly acted as consultant and helped me to avoid many errors and insensitivities. Sikhs in Australia, especially Kuldip and Sarjit Singh's family, as well as Darshan Singh, Mohinder Singh's family, Jit's and Gurpreet and Baljeet Singh's in India, Rani Kaur and Pavi Singh's, Narinder Kapany's, and Kuldip and Carol Sethi's in the USA, Jarnail Singh's in Canada, and Sikh friends too many to mention in Britain have also provided help, knowingly or unwittingly, and wonderful hospitality.

Professor Hew McLeod has been a friend and helper over many years, always ready speedily to answer queries. Pal Singh Purewal has interpreted the Nanakshahi Calender to me.

Richard Ball Publishing kindly agreed to my use of material from my 'A' level sample answers. Amrit and Rabindra Kaur of Twin Studios have enhanced the book with their illustrations and I am very grateful to them for putting their considerable artistic talents at my disposal and for being so patient. The photographs on pages 12, 29, 37, 49, 59, 72 and 86 were provided by Harjinder Singh Sagoo of Photographic Services and to him too I must express my appreciation for many years of friendship and professional help. Annette Voss kindly supplied the nagar kirtan photograph on page 192. I am grateful to Joy Barrow for help in using the Internet.

My greatest debt of gratitude, however, as always, is owed to

Gwynneth for 45 years of love, and good humoured encouragement and support.

Despite the best efforts of Catherine Coe and her colleagues at Hodder & Stoughton readers are likely to discover errors. They are my responsibility only. If they are pointed out to me, I will try to correct them in later editions.

Owen Cole

dedication

My late friend Piara Singh Sambhi and his Virdi and Sambhi families, wherever I have met them, have always honoured me as their brother, and my family as their kin. There are no words or deeds that can possibly express my gratitude to them sufficiently for this, and all their many kindnesses, over 25 years. Perhaps this book, which contains so much that I learned from being with them in what has become my second home, might be accepted as a small token of gratitude and affection.

contents

author's introduction

Books on religions are often necessarily factual and academic. In this study of the Sikh religion the attempt has been made to enter as fully as possible into the life and faith, as well as beliefs, of Sikhs so that readers may be able to appreciate what it means to be a Sikh. It is only possible to achieve limited success in this endeavour. Those who wish to go further must, as I do, walk with Sikhs and enjoy their sorrows and joys. If this book has helped a single reader to embark upon the experiences and friendships that I have had, or to respect the faith that is held by followers of the Gurus, or merely to understand it, then it will have succeeded in its purpose.

W. Owen Cole, February 2003
University College, Chichester

Vaisaki 2003,
Nanakshahi 535

The publishers wish to thank Twin Studio for supplying artwork, Harjinder Singh Sagoo and Annette Voss for supplying those photographs listed in the Acknowledgements, and Dr W Owen Cole for supplying the remaining photographs.

Every effort has been made to trace and acknowledge ownership of copyright. The publishers will be glad to make suitable arrangements with any copyright holders whom it has not been possible to contact.

01

introduction: worship

In this chapter you will learn:

- about the key Sikh activity, congregational worship
- about gurdwaras in the diaspora
- functionaries in what is essentially a non-hierarchical religion.

This photograph shows the kind of scene you would see if you entered a Sikh place of worship, a *gurdwara*, almost anywhere in the world.

Notice the following:

- the ornate canopy and the posts that support it
- the woman sitting below the canopy, holding a fan (*chauri*)
- the musicians with their Indian instruments
- a man preparing to bow
- people sitting on the floor, men and women separate, not all the men are wearing turbans, though everyone's head is covered. (The women are out of picture, on the right.)

From your initial observations you can deduce a number of things about the Sikh religion.

The seated woman may have led you to conclude that women are people of some importance. You would be right. In fact, women and men have equal standing. Either may lead worship or any other religious activity, so long as they have the necessary competence, such as the ability to read the scripture, the Guru Granth Sahib.

The musicians, known as *ragis,* inform you that Sikh worship attaches importance to music. Not all religions do but it is an integral part of Sikh worship. The instruments provide a clue to the Indian origins of Sikhism; notice that women are among the instrumentalists.

Sikhs bring offerings of money to the gurdwara but, because a shared meal, known as *langar,* is an essential part of worship, they also bring food to use in it. (These offerings cannot be seen clearly in the photograph on page 2.)

Everyone sits on the floor to show the equality of all human beings; this included Prince Charles, the Prince of Wales, when he visited a gurdwara in Derby. Respect for the scripture is the main reason why Sikhs sit on the floor in the gurdwara. It alone is given a seat of honour. In its presence every head must be covered as another mark of respect. Not all male Sikhs wear a turban. Those who do not, and other visitors, usually tie a handkerchief over the head. No one wears shoes, but stockinged feet are permitted in all but a few major gurdwaras. Every Sikh takes a bath before going to the gurdwara; this is another way of honouring the scripture. Men and women sit in separate groups on the ground because in Indian society it is not considered modest for them to sit together in conditions that must inevitably result in physical contact, particularly on occasions when the hall is filled to capacity.

In some parts of the Sikh dispersion (that is, in communities outside India) there has been discussion about introducing chairs into the hall where worship takes place. So far this attempt at modernization has been resisted. Most Sikhs are likely to regard it more as a challenge to the unique position of the scripture than a move to bring Sikhism up to date. So strongly do Sikhs feel about this that even those who walk with the aid of crutches are likely to prefer to sit propped against the wall, rather than ask to be allowed to use a chair, though Sikhs are often eager to invite disabled visitors to sit on one at the back of the hall rather than be uncomfortable.

Part of Sikh worship is the langar meal, which will be discussed later. In India this invariably is eaten by Sikhs sitting on the ground. In the West, chairs and tables may be used. Some Western gurdwaras have reverted to the Punjabi custom, but in this case the reason has to do with long established tradition rather than belief in equality which is taken for granted.

From what has been written already you will have realized that the Guru Granth Sahib (the Sikh holy book) has special importance for Sikhs. It is not very clearly visible in the photograph but it is its focal point. The woman is reading the scripture. She is holding a fan of yak hair embedded in silver, a chauri, in her hand and occasionally waves it over the Guru Granth Sahib in a gesture of respect. The canopy, *chanani*, serves the same purpose. The throne used by the British queen at the state opening of parliament has a canopy. When she visits an eastern country, an umbrella may be held over her head, not only for the practical purpose of sheltering her from sun or rain, but in response to her status.

By now you may have realized that the scripture is seated on a throne, rather like one used by princes of Mughal emperors in India in past times. When Sikhs approach the throne, on entering the gurdwara, they bow and kneel in front of it before sitting facing it in the congregation, *sangat*. The act of worship Sikhs engage in is called *diwan*, the word used for an audience with a Mughal emperor. The room of the gurdwara in which worship is held is known as the diwan hall.

The equality of Sikhs is further demonstrated through the use of food. At the end of an act of worship, every member of the sangat, whether they be adults, children, or visitors who are not Sikhs receives *karah parshad*. This is made of flour, sugar and ghee, mixed in equal quantities in an iron bowl, and then heated before being carried into the diwan hall, perhaps before the service begins, but certainly before six stanzas of the Anand, a hymn of thanksgiving, are chanted. Before distribution it is touched with the point of a *kirpan*, a short sword which initiated Sikhs wear, to strengthen it symbolically, and given to five initiated Sikhs before being served to the rest of the congregation. Though it is usually received at the end of worship in Britain, in large Indian gurdwaras where worship continues throughout the day, Sikhs may be given it after bowing to the Guru Granth Sahib, or upon leaving its presence. During diwan, in another room of the gurdwara, some Sikhs will have been preparing food. A community meal called *langar* is another way of affirming the belief of Sikhs in the equality of everyone. Sikhism came to birth in a Hindu society where almost all people ate only with members of their own kinship or occupational group. They believed in ritual pollution, that is that by sharing food with men lower in the social hierarchy, and perhaps any women, especially during menstruation, they would be rendered impure and unable to approach God. The men who preached the message of Sikhism totally rejected this belief and used karah parshad and langar as practical ways of demonstrating this. Anyone may eat with Sikhs, their kitchen is open to all, but those who have reservations or misgivings about human equality will refuse the invitation to eat with them. Sikhs would not interpret it as a dislike of hot Indian food, but as a refusal to eat with them for some reason. In their attempt to offend no one, the food provided at langar is always vegetarian, usually a simple meal of lentil soup (dahl), vegetables, rice and chappatis.

Sikhs are very fond of telling the story of the Mughal emperor Akbar the Great who made a visit to one of the Sikh leaders, Guru Amar Das. Before being allowed into the Guru's presence, the emperor was required to sit on the ground and share food with other men and women. 'Pehle pangat, piche sangat', first eat together then worship together, is a major tenet of Sikh faith. God is no respecter of persons and those who would wish to meet God cannot hope to do so unless they regard all human beings as God does. The photograph with which this chapter began could have been taken almost anywhere in the world. However, there are some variations which might be encountered from place to place, though not usually in the act of worship itself.

Chairs and tables are often used in the dispersion for langar which will be eaten indoors in countries like Britain, whereas in India it is often served outdoors, perhaps on leaf plates with people sitting in rows on the ground. The food served the world over remains Punjabi. The meal is satisfying and enjoyable but is intended to sustain and remove hunger as well as express unity rather than offer five-star sophisticated Indian cuisine. In India, pilgrims of all religions and other travellers often take langar in the gurdwaras that lie on their route, knowing that Sikhs are under obligation to give hospitality to anyone who asks for it. This may include accommodation for the night. Many of the larger gurdwaras have guest rooms where up to three nights' stay may be provided. After this the traveller should be fully rested and able to continue his journey. (Indian women would rarely, if ever, travel alone.)

Members of the sangat provide the food, prepare it, serve it, and do the washing-up afterwards. When a family has a particular event to celebrate they may request the opportunity to express their joy through the privilege of providing langar for the congregation.

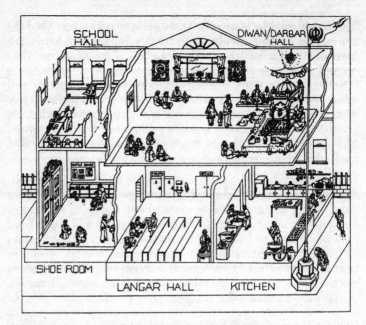

figure 1 cut away illustration of a purpose built gurdwara in one of the countries of the Sikh dispersion

In India, the extended family will share the work among themselves, elsewhere they may call upon the help of friends.

Because the Sikh scriptures are in Punjabi, and Sikhs have a strong attachment to that region of India even though they may have lived abroad for three or four generations, Punjabi remains the language of worship everywhere. The time is likely to come when Sikhs use the language of the country in which they live for sermons and addresses but it has not arrived yet, and the scriptures will always be recited in the original language in Sikh worship. It is not possible to envisage a translation of the Guru Granth Sahib ever being installed as the focus of worship.

The content and purpose of Sikh worship

We have noted the principal features of the gurdwara and some of the activities that take place there. The main one is worship which will now be examined in more detail.

The purpose of Sikh worship is to praise God and develop the spirituality of the individual and the community. God does not need our praise, which is what worship is for Sikhs. It is the natural response of the one who is the recipient of grace to the one who gives it, God. It is offered by those who are awesomely aware of God within creation, as well as within individual human hearts. Corporate worship in the gurdwara, diwan, it should be noted, however, is only one aspect of Sikh worship. Its form is simple, the singing of hymns from the Guru Granth Sahib, led by musicians, ragis, and a series of addresses, *kathas*, based on them.

In places where the local sangat is large enough to sustain it, the Guru Granth Sahib will be formally installed in the early morning at the ceremony of Parkash Karna which is described on page 119. Sikhs will come to pay their respects to it at various times during the day, especially before and after work. God is to be praised at all times and kept constantly in mind. Bowing to the scripture, the Guru Granth Sahib, is an outward sign of praising God whose word it contains.

In Britain, Sunday is the most convenient time for congregational worship but Sikhs do not consider any time or occasion better than another. Many Sikhs will touch the gurdwara steps and then their foreheads as they enter the building, as they would the feet of Gurus in the past. This act of *māatthā teknā* is a way of showing respect to God whose house the gurdwara is. So, too is the prostration or bow they make when they approach the Guru Granth Sahib. The removal of shoes before entering the prayer hall has the same meaning. These actions are part of everyday Indian life but in the gurdwara their significance is that of recognizing and responding to the unique sovereignty of God.

The scripture (*bani*) is God's word. It inspires and commands Sikhs, giving spiritual comfort and discipline of mind and spirit. A few lines near the end of the Guru Granth Sahib, written by the fifth Sikh teacher, Guru Arjan, and called Mundavani, the Seal, state the Sikh belief clearly. They read:

> In the platter are placed three things: truth, contentment and wisdom, as well as God's Name, the support of all. Whoever eats this food, whoever relishes it, is emanicipated.

The Sikh worshiper hopes to be nourished by God's word.

The conclusion of diwan

Whatever the general content of diwan, the conclusion is always as follows:

- Six verses of The Anand Sahib of Guru Amar Das which read:

1 *O joy, my mother, I have found the True Guru. I have found the True Guru and songs of rejoicing fill my heart. Beautiful songs and heavenly singers come to sing praises to God. Those who keep God within ever sing God's praises. Nanak says, my heart is full of joy, for I have found the True Guru.*

2 *O my soul, live with God forever. Abide with God and all your sorrows will vanish. You will be acceptable to God who will take charge of all your affairs. The Perfect One is omnipotent; why forget God? Nanak says, live with God forever.*

3 *O my True One, is there anything that your house does not contain? Everything is in your house, there for whoever you decide to give it to. The recipient will praise your bounty and honour your name. Strains of heavenly music resound for one in whose heart your name resides. Says Nanak, is there anything that your house does not contain?*

4 *The True Name sustains me forever. The True Name satisfies my hunger and sustains me. God's name is awakened in my heart. It has given me peace and joy and fulfilled all my desires. I will always be a sacrifice to the Guru who displays such kindness. Says Nanak, listen O saints, love the Word. The True Name sustains me forever.*

5 *Celestial music rings through the house. Music resounds in the house where God's might has been infused. There God has conquered the five passions and destroyed fear of death. Those favoured by destiny are attached to God's Name. Nanak says, they have found happiness and they hear celestial music in their hearts.*

40 *Listen to my joy, my fortunate friends. All my desires have been fulfilled. I have attained to God the Supreme Spirit and all my sorrows have vanished. Sorrow, affliction and suffering have been dispelled through hearing the true Word. Saints and holy people are glad on hearing it from the perfect Guru.*

Pure are the hearers; starless the speakers; the True Guru will fill their hearts. Nanak says, heavenly trumpets sound for those who bow at the Guru's feet.

- Some words from Guru Nanak's *Japji*, a hymn so important that it is given pride of place at the beginning of the Guru Granth Sahib.

  Air, water, and earth, these are the elements from which we are made. Air, like the Guru's Word, gives breath to life to the baby born to the great mother earth, sired by the waters. Night and day are the nurses which watch over us in our infancy. We play in their lap. The world is our playground. Our right and wrong acts will receive judgement in your court. Some will be seated near your throne and some far away. Toil has ended for those who worship you. O Nanak, their faces are radiant with joy. They free many others.

- A section of the *Sukhmani Sahib* (Hymn of Peace) of Guru Arjan.

  You are the Supreme One; I pray to you. My body and soul are the gifts for starting life. You are both father and mother, we are your children. We draw many blessings from your grace. No one knows your limits; you are the highest of the high. All creation depends on your will; it has to accept all that comes from you. You alone know what determines your purpose. I am ever a sacrifice to you.

- *Ardas* is then offered by a member of the congregation. This congregational prayer, which is used at any assembly of Sikhs as well as in private devotions, calls to mind the Gurus, important incidents in Sikh history, and ends with the needs of the sangat in which the prayer is said. Ardas indicates that there is a place for petitionary prayer in Sikhism. It also unites Sikhs with the Panth (the community of Sikhs worldwide past and present), and looks towards the future. It reads:

  Victory to the Eternal One. May almighty God protect us.

  First remember almighty God, then call to mind Guru Nanak, Guru Angad, Guru Amar Das and Guru Ram Das, may they help us. Remember Gurus Arjan,

Hargobind, Har Rai and Har Krishan whose sight removes all sorrows. May we remember Guru Tegh Bahadur at whose invocation the nine treasures [spiritual blessings] come hastening to our homes. May they help and protect us at all times.

May we always enjoy the protection of the Tenth Guru, Guru Gobind Singh. Disciples of the Gurus, meditate on the Guru Granth Sahib, the visible form of the Guru. Repeat in the name of God. Vahiguru.[1]

Think of the glorious deeds of the five beloved ones, (panj piare[2]) the Guru's four sons,[3] the forty liberated ones,[4] and other who were steadfast and long-suffering. Remember them and call on God. Vahiguru.

Call to mind those who kept the Name in their hearts and shared their earnings with others. Vahiguru.
Those who allowed themselves to be cut limb from limb, had their scalps scraped off, were broken on the wheel, were sawn or flayed alive, remember them. Vahiguru.

Think of those who cleansed the gurdwaras, permitted themselves to be beaten, imprisoned, shot, maimed or burned alive with neither resistance nor complaint, and call on God. Vahiguru.

As you remember the seats of authority (takhts[5]) and other places touched by the Gurus' feet, call on God. Vahiguru.

May the whole Khalsa remember the Wonderful One, and as it does so may it be blessed. May God's protection be upon all members of the Khalsa wherever they may be, and God's glory be proclaimed and way prevail.

May the Khalsa be victorious in battle. Uphold its charitable acts and let victory attend it. May the Khalsa choirs, flags and mansions remain forever. May the kingdom of justice come. May Sikhs be united in love and humility, but exalted in the wisdom of remembering God. O Khalsa, say Vahiguru. Vahiguru.

O true king and loving father, we have sung your sweet hymns, heard your word which gives life and talked of your many blessings. May these find a place in our hearts so that our souls may be drawn towards you. O Father, save us from lust, anger, greed, worldly attachment and pride: keep us always attached to your feet. Grant to your Sikhs the gift of discipleship, the gift of your Name, the gift of faith, the gift of reading your word with understanding. O kind and loving father, through your mercy we have passed our days in peace and happiness: grant that we may be obedient to your will. Give us light and understanding so that we may please you. We offer this prayer in your presence, Wonderful One. Forgive us our wrong acts, help us to remain pure. Bring us into the good company of those who love you and remember your Name. Through Nanak may the glory of your Name increase and may the whole world be blessed by your grace. Vahiguru ji ka Khalsa! Vahiguruji ki fateh. Sat Sri Akal![6]

Notes

The content of Ardas, the Sikh congregational prayer, varies considerably. The form given above is that found in Cole and Sambhi, 1995, Appendix 2. Teja Singh, 1938, provides another but similar version. See also McLeod, 1990: 103–5.

1 Vahiguru means literally, 'Praise to the Guru'. It is also used as a popular way of addressing or speaking about God.
2 The panj piare were the first five Sikhs to be initiated into the Khalsa (see page 35).
3 Guru Gobind Singh's four sons who were all killed in the struggle against the Mughals.
4 These were deserters who were forgiven by Guru Gobind Singh and later fell in battle as soldiers in his army.
5 The five seats of religious authority (see pages 152f).
6 These words are often uttered before or after a Sikh speaks in the gurdwara and on other occasions. They mean 'Hail to the Guru's Khalsa! Hail to the victory of the Guru! God is True!' The acclamation is also an affirmation of community agreement, for example at the end of a discussion in the gurdwara.

There then follows a random opening of the Guru Granth Sahib. The passage (*vak*) is read aloud to the congregation. They regard it as the Guru's instruction and command (*hukam*) for the day that lies ahead. Karah parshad will be shared. The congregation may then disperse for langar or notices and sangat business may be conducted.

figure 2 the distribution of karah parshad by women as well as men is a way of demonstrating the equality of women and men

Karah parshad must be included in worship. This *halwa* or pudding is sweet to signify God's grace, as well as symbolizing human equality. Everyone should accept it, regardless of social group. Those who reject it thereby refuse grace and invalidate their worship.

The langar meal is also an integral part of worship. It, too, symbolizes the provident grace of God as well as the openness of Sikhs to all people. Anyone may receive langar and Sikhs would be offended should anyone refuse. In the context of worship, karah parshad and langar are declarations that God's love is available to everyone and no one has the right to deny it. Congregational worship emphasizes equality in another way. Women may participate fully in all its aspects. There are no theological reasons for barring women from taking the lead in any religious activity. On the contrary, Sikh teaching positively endorses the spiritual and religious equality of women with men.

Congregational worship is fundamental to Sikhism. There is no such thing as a Sikh who pursues the path of individual spirituality as an ascetic or a recluse. The Gurus derived spiritual strength from the sangat to which they often expressed their indebtedness. Corporate worship owes its *raison d'être* to the practice of the Gurus.

Visiting a gurdwara in the dispora

- Carry no tobacco or alcohol.
- Remove shoes, cover head. As you will be sitting on the floor it would be sensible to wear long skirts or trousers. Bare shoulders or arms are likely to cause offence.
- Sikhs will kneel in front of the Guru Granth Sahib and bow their heads until it touches the ground. They will also place a small offering in a box or on the ground.

Visitors may follow this practice but at the very least they should stand and bow towards the scripture before taking their place among the other women or men who will be sitting separately in the congregation.

ARRANGING A VISIT

This is best done through personal contact rather than only by phone call or letter. The purpose of the visit can then be explained and, perhaps, the opportunity taken to view the building in preparation for taking a group of children or adults. Contact with a person known by name can be helpful.

The availability of toilets is a practical matter of importance! Parking may be another.

If you are planning to make a visit on your own you will be most welcome to go any Sunday (the most convenient day. About 11.00 a.m. might be a good time. You can 'drop in' but you and your hosts might feel more comfortable if the first visit is by prior arrangement).

You should, of course, accept karah parshad and take langar. Never be in a hurry!

Private devotion through daily *nam simran* (meditation) is as essential as congregational worship, so is the service of humanity. Unless God is seen in every heart, divinity cannot be found in one's own. Hence the emphasis upon *seva*, service. This may take many forms but the Sikh Code of Discipline, the Rahit

Maryada, in its section on langar states that the gurdwara is the school in which one learns to serve humanity. Often the beginning is made by serving food, washing-up and removing the litter but these activities are no less worship than singing God's praises or playing the musical instruments that accompany the singing.

Sikh worship is more than an act of praising God in the gurdwara daily, or less frequently with other Sikhs. Living, for the Sikh, should be an act of worship.

Two symbols are likely to be seen in gurdwaras. One is the *khanda*.

This is formed of an upright double-edged sword, called a khanda, circled by a *chakra*, with two swords (kirpans) to either side. A number of symbolic meanings are given to each of these three elements. This is only one of them. The double-edged sword has blades that must be equally honed, otherwise its balance is lost and it is useless. It reminds Sikhs that Guru Gobind Singh taught them that members of the Khalsa should be saint-soldiers, women and men who balance skill in arms with spirituality. The kirpans remind Sikhs of Guru Arjan's instruction to his son, Guru Hargobind, that he should wear two swords, one of *piri*, spiritual power, and the other of *miri*, temporal authority. The chakra, a throwing weapon, is an ancient Indian symbol which, for Sikhs, speaks of the oneness of God, the unity of humanity, and, implicitly, the rejection of caste, racial, and gender divisions.

The khanda is to be seen on the *nishan sahib*, the yellow or saffron flag that flies over every gurdwara. It also often adorns the canopy over the Guru Granth Sahib.

Ik Oankar is the other Sikh symbol.

Ik is the figure one. The word oankar is the equivalent of the sanskrit '*Om*' and, like it, represents God. 'Ik oankar' is also the first statement of the *Mul Mantra* and thus reminds Sikhs of that important affirmation of belief. Ik oankar may well be found on the canopy above the Guru Granth Sahib, or on the *rumalas*, the decorated cloths that Sikhs give as coverings for the scripture.

Sikh functionaries

Whenever the Guru Granth Sahib lies open it will be attended by a male or a female Sikh. This could be anyone who is capable of reading it and is, of course, in good standing within the community.

In the Sikh religion everyone is equal to the extend that there are no officials set apart for life to lead worship or organize the community and the religion. People who are appointed to any special positions do not have a job for life. When their particular duty is over they revert to being members of the community.

Sikh ministry is uncomplicated and straightforward. It derives from Guru Nanak's teaching on the oneness of God and the indivisible unity of humanity. In Sikhism there is no priest–laity distinction. The very notion of a priesthood is alien to Sikhs who belong to a movement that long ago rejected the authority and ritual specialization of the *brahmins*. Every aspect of ministry is open to all Sikhs, both men and women, though, of course, only Khalsa Sikhs may conduct the initiation ceremonies (see Chapter 03).

The student of Sikhism may soon come across the terms '*granthi*', '*giani*' and also '*sant*'. Sometimes the first two may be used synonymously and are mistakenly translated into English as 'priest' by Sikhs who wish to be helpful, but actually cause confusion, and may even create a certain suspicion in the minds of some protestant, anti-clerical Christians, of whom a few still exist! However, strictly speaking a granthi is only the custodian and reader of the Guru Granth Sahib and, by extension, may look after a gurdwara, though a committee will manage its affairs and appoint a granthi if there is one. S/he, though I have never yet met a female granthi, will officiate at weddings and other ceremonies. Some wealthy gurdwaras may employ several granthis to organize and lead the religious life of the community, which begins before dawn and continues without a break until 9.00 or 10.00 p.m. (In the Golden Temple of Amritsar, worship ceases only from about 10.00 p.m. until 3.00 a.m.) Other gurdwaras in the West, which serve a community of only 100 or so people, may open only from about noon on a Sunday until 3.00 p.m. They cannot afford, and really do not need, a granthi, though often the pride of the local sangat means that it aspires to appointing one as soon as possible and opening the gurdwara for Sikhs to be able to attend every evening, if not at other times of the day.

Traditionally, a giani is a person of spiritual knowledge who has achieved unity with God, someone who is *brahmgiani*, filled with divine understanding. It is also an academic qualification in Punjabi language and literature, possibly, though not always, including the Sikh scriptures. A granthi may sometimes be respectfully addressed as *gianiji* just to complicate matters, without any implication of knowledge being intended! '*Bhai sahib*', which literally means brother, is a more usual respectful title.

A *sant* is a preceptor who has gained a reputation as a teacher and spiritual guide. For this reason they are given the title sant. In the scriptures a sant is an enlightened individual. Sant may be used as a prefix to a Sikh's name, for example Sant Puran Singh. The title has no formal validity. Their spirituality and knowledge of Sikh teachings (*gurmat*) is so considerably developed that they acquire a respect and with it a following of devotees similar to that enjoyed by Hindu gurus. Sants are influential guides who assist those who come to them in organizing their spiritual and everyday lives. They may have a *dehra*, an encampment or group of houses, which some Sikhs visit occasionally but where others stay more permanently. Followers may be encouraged to adopt strict regimes which will usually have taking *amrit* at the centre, but may also stress vegetarianism and periods of celibacy. Sants may travel internationally with their closest companions by invitation, or as missionaries to sangats abroad.

The line between a sant and a Namdhari or Sikh Nirankari Guru can become very indistinct in practice. The true sant, however, should always point Sikhs away from himself and towards the teachings of the Gurus.

Sikh greetings

When Sikhs meet they may shake hands following the custom of the West, acquired from the British. They will invariably shake hands with someone like myself, so I need not wonder, as I often do nowadays in British society, whether it is expected or not. When I meet a Sikh man it is expected. Sikhs may press their hands together as they bow slightly towards another person of Indian origin whom they are greeting. If they are close friends or relatives they will embrace one another. It is unlikely that there will be any body contact between men and women unless they are related, in which case an uncle may pat his niece on the shoulder. Kissing is not acceptable and would never take place in public.

A difficult situation can arise when someone like myself is introduced to a Sikh lady. Do I shake hands or not? In Britain, and occasionally in India, I might be expected to do so, but the proper custom is to press my hands together, bow slightly, smile and say 'Sat Sri Akal', as a Sikh would. This is the recommended form of behaviour. It will be appreciated because it shows that you have taken the trouble to discover something about Sikh culture. If you take the initiative it also anticipates, and so avoids, any possibility of embarrassment. 'Sat Sri Akal' means 'Truth is eternal'. It reminds the people who utter it that they should try to live truthfully.

When someone addresses the sangat they are likely to begin by saying: 'Vahiguruji ka Khalsa, vahiguruji ki fateh', which means something to the effect of 'The Khalsa belongs to God (Vahiguru), may victory be God's'. When someone's words win the acclaim of the sangat it is likely to be greeted with someone shouting 'Jo Bolé So Nihal'. To which everyone responds 'Sat Sri Akal'. The cry is said to be difficult to translate. It is a slogan of approval endorsed by the sangat. Sometimes the speaker may say, instead 'Sat Sangat, Khalsa ji', 'Members of the congregation and Khalsa . . .'

The sangat may confer a *saropa*, literally a robe, upon a person who has served them, perhaps an architect who has planned a building or a local clergy person who has promoted good Sikh–Christian relations. It is likely to take the form of a turban length, or even, but rarely in Britain, a sword. Sometimes sangats depart from the tradition by giving the honoured person books that will help them to understand the Sikhs and their religion better. If the recipient feels able to speak for about five minutes on such a subject as the contribution that Sikhs are making to the locality, for example, it will be appreciated by the congregation, probably in the manner mentioned in the previous paragraph.

02
the beginnings of Sikhism

In this chapter you will learn:

- about the origins of Sikhism
- about its attitudes to its religious context
- about the role of Guru Nanak.

If you were to visit a Sikh home anywhere in the world you would be likely to see a number of pictures on the walls of most rooms. They may be identical in size to some that were displayed in the gurdwara, or they may be much smaller. Almost certainly one would be of a man wearing a turban, whose long white beard enhances his rather benign expression. This is Guru Nanak, the founder of the Sikh religion. Of course, no one knows what he actually looked like. In common with other great religious teachers of the past, such as the Buddha, Jesus or Muhammad, it was their message that mattered, not their physical appearance. Nanak was born in the area of north India known as Punjab just over 500 years ago, 1469.

The great invasion of the Mughal leader Babur still lay 50 years in the future, but Muslims had penetrated and settled in Punjab during the centuries before Nanak's birth and his father, Kalu, was employed as village accountant by a local landlord, the Muslim Rai Bular. The village of Talvandi must have been like many others in the region, inhabited mainly by Hindus but with most wealth and power residing in Muslim hands. Biographical knowledge of Guru Nanak is confined to a number of collections called *janam sakhis*. Their purpose was to create and sustain faith, not primarily to provide historical information. In fact, Guru Nanak and his successors frequently pointed their followers away from devotion to themselves to trust in the spiritually liberating words that they uttered, which are included in the pages of the Sikh scriptures.

Was Nanak a Hindu?

The obvious answer to this question would seem to be 'yes', but it is not the Sikh answer. Sikhs would point to the stories surrounding his birth and early childhood such as that describing the casting of his horoscope by the family priest, Pandit Hardyal, who said:

> Both Hindus and Muslims will pay him reverence. His name will become current on earth and in heaven. The ocean will give way to him, so will the earth and skies. He will worship and acknowledge only the one formless Lord, and teach others to do so.

The child's spiritual qualities won the approval of Hindu and Muslim alike. A Hindu passing by would involuntarily exclaim, 'Great is Gobind the Lord! Such a small child and yet he speaks so auspiciously. His words are as immaculate as he is handsome. He is the image of God himself!' And if a Muslim saw him he would remark with equal enthusiasm, 'Wonderful is thy creation, Merciful Master! How good looking is the child, how polite in his speech! Talking to him brings one such satisfaction. He is a noble one blessed by Allah himself.'

When he was some years older, but still a child, the time came for Nanak to be invested with the sacred thread, as his family belonged to one of the higher Hindu castes. He asked the priest whether he was able to give him a thread which would not wear out, some permanent spiritual gift. This the priest admitted that he was unable to do.

Nanak continued to be a troublesome young man in his family's eyes, even though his spiritual qualities were recognized and valued by others. He followed his father into accountancy, which was the custom of the day, but showed little aptitude for it. 'Tera' (13) is a lucky number for Sikhs, (though, like other people who believe in God, luck should have no place in their thinking). 'Tera' also means 'yours'. For Nanak it spoke of his commitment to God, 'I am yours'. In his counting he could proceed no further but went into deep meditation.

At last his despairing parents sent him to stay with Nanaki, his married sister, at Sultanpur. Her husband Jai Ram found him accountancy work in the Muslim nawab's grainstore. One day, while he was at Sultanpur, Nanak did not return from his early ablutions in the nearby river Bein. Three days later he returned to the village. In the interval he had been communing with the Supreme Being. As one account states:

> As the Primal Being willed, Nanak, the devotee, was ushered into the Divine Presence. Then a cup filled with nectar (amrit) was given him with the command, 'This is the cup of Name-Adoration. Drink it . . . I am with you and I bless you and exalt you. Whoever remembers you will enjoy my favour. Go, rejoice in my Name and teach others to do so . . . I have bestowed on you the gift of my Name. Let this be your calling'. Nanak offered his salutations and stood up.

On his return to Sultanpur Nanak, when he eventually broke his silence, said,

> There is no Hindu and no Mussulman (Muslim), so whose path (system of teaching) shall I follow? God is

*neither Hindu nor Mussulman and the path I shall
follow is God's.*

An attempt to explain the meaning of this astonishing statement
might be regarded as the subplot of this book but, returning to
our question 'Was Guru Nanak a Hindu', we can begin to see
that Sikhs regard him as one who does not fit into the category
of Hindu. He transcended the limits of sixteenth-century India
sectarianism, not necessarily repudiating the two systems but
certainly not being enchained by them. From this time onwards,
he was known not as 'Nanak' but 'Guru Nanak', a title which
Sikhs always give to him, capitalizing the 'G'.

The place of the Guru in Hinduism

This is not the place for a detailed study of this important Hindu
teaching but some awareness of it is necessary if the word Guru,
when referred to the Sikh Gurus, is to be understood.

A very important feature of Hinduism is the emphasis upon
spiritual experience. The word guru is often explained by
splitting it into two parts. Gu- means darkness and ru- means
light. A guru is one who dispels spiritual darkness and gives light
to the disciple (called a *chela* or *sishya*, for which the Punjabi
equivalent is 'Sikh'). Guru can also be linked with a word
meaning heavy. He is a person who removes the burden of doubt
and ignorance which the disciple brings as the consequence of
karma.

To be effective, a guru must traditionally possess four essential
qualities. He must be *shratiya*, well versed in the scriptures. He
must be *brahmanishtam*, established in brahman. This means he
must have realized the spiritual goal himself. He must be
akamakita, unsmitten by desire. He must be stainless, free from
guile. Only such a person can enable the seeker to achieve
liberation. As the guru Chaitanya (1486–1533) said:

> *The guru is the skilful helmsman, divine grace the
> favourable wind; if with such means a man does not
> strive to cross the ocean of life and death, he is indeed
> lost.*

A helmsman who does not know the way across the ocean of
birth and rebirth, *samsara*, is worse than useless.

Hinduism teaches that God, brahman, is within everyone but that the natural state of humanity is one in which this awareness is made impossible through ignorance. The guru is convinced of a divine vocation.

The *chela* is equally sure of the guru's ability to enable him to achieve the same status of *brahma vidya*, knowledge which is intuitive as well as intellectual, the realization of brahman.

As the words of Chaitanya state, the guru is essential to the achievements of *moksha*. Many Hindus attach great significance to the fact that the guru is a brahmin whose teaching is based on the Vedas (Hindu scriptures), but for some it is not orthodoxy of teaching that matters but how the guru matches up to the devotee's prayer expressed in the Brihadaranyaka Upanishad:

> *From the unreal lead me to the real, from darkness lead me to light, from death lead me to immortality.*

Guru Nanak's success is attributable to the fact that those who listened to him felt that his teaching was authentic. His words and his lifestyle possessed a coherence and integrity that was missing in some other men who claimed to be gurus.

The North India religious situation as Guru Nanak perceived it

There are two ways of looking at everything, a right way and a wrong way, some people say. This is certainly not the case when examining the teachings of Guru Nanak about Hinduism and Islam. He is often dismissive, as we shall see, but he is also affirmative. Apparently, it is possible to achieve spiritual liberation from material existence through being Hindu or Muslim, but not easy.

Guru Nanak spoke out strongly against a number of particular aspects of Hinduism but perhaps his condemnation can be summed up in one word – divisiveness. Of course, the contrary argument can be put that Hinduism is a unifying system, but this is not how Guru Nanak saw it and in this book it is the Sikh view that is being expressed and analysed.

He was acutely aware of living in a society fragmented not only by the rivalry of two religions but by a Hindu religion which, in his view, effectively taught social disunity and religious segregation, giving little or no hope of spiritual liberation to most villagers. He had a clear view of one spiritual reality immanent in all creation and therefore in every person. Hinduism, for him, did not affirm the rich diversity of the One spiritual reality in speaking of its many forms: it taught polytheism and the worship of idols, and, through one particular concept, denied the unity of human kind.

Pollution

We cannot go far in an attempt to understand Sikh teaching without being aware of a key Hindu concept, that of pollution. This has nothing to do with dirt and the environmental issues that concern us in the twenty-first century. The river Ganges at Banares is as polluted as the Tyne was in my childhood, when I was warned not to fall into it for I would certainly catch things from it that would kill me. Yet the Ganges is pure, and the source of purification for all who bathe in it – with sincere pious motives, of course. Certain places and seasons are pure. The higher the caste, the more pure a person is. Brahmins are almost naturally pure. If they incur impurity from bodily contact with an impure person, with a corpse, or through sexual intercourse, for example, they can regain their status of purity by bathing or performing other rituals. The Hindus who used to be called 'untouchables' are people at the other end of the spectrum, living in a state of permanent impurity. To touch them or things with which they have been in contact results in pollution.

Hinduism has always had its critics of the concept of ritual pollution. Mahatma Gandhi is one of the most recent examples, and the Hindu tradition itself changes. Being jostled together on a bus, or confronted by a professor or bank manager who is of low caste may stimulate reflection upon traditional concepts of superiority. The *kala pani*, black water, is something no Hindu should cross for fear of pollution, but there are some 550,000 Hindus living in Britain, not to mention Indonesia, the Caribbean, and the USA. I once met a brahmin who asked where I had learned about Hinduism. When I told him, 'In Britain', he said that was impossible, there could be no Hindus in Britain. He meant either that by crossing the Black Ocean they had ceased to be Hindus or, more likely, that no true Hindu would even contemplate travelling beyond the pure land of India.

Ritual pollution and purity are not concepts unique to Hinduism. They are clearly found in Judaism and Islam, as well as some forms of Buddhism. In Christianity, the notion of sacred places implies that others are profane, especially when such buildings as churches are specially consecrated and the Mass or Eucharist has to be conducted by persons set apart for the purpose. When additional emphasis is placed upon these officiants being celibate and male (to avoid the pollution of menstruation), then the importance of ritual purity for many Christians, though they may have become unaware of it through familiarity, becomes obvious. Perhaps no more need be said, but the Christian view of the Blessed Virgin Mary might be a fruitful area for further exploration.

Ritual pollution for Guru Nanak, led to a society in which the brahmin priests would only minister to those who belonged to the three upper classes of brahmin, kshatriya and vaishya; where women of any class were excluded because menstruation and childbirth, both involving blood, rendered them impure. The six recognized philosophical systems of Hindu teaching, based on the most important Hindu texts, the Vedas, did not provide alternative but equally acceptable paths to liberation – they each claimed to be the only one capable of helping men to achieve that goal, which was, of course, closed to all women.

The following passages provide some illustrations of his criticism.

> *If the principle of impurity is admitted, then impurity is everywhere. There are worms in cow dung and in wood. Many though the grains of corn be, there is none of them which does not contain life. There was life in the primordial waters from which vegetation came. How can impurity be warded off? It is to be found in every kitchen. Nanak says, pollution is not removed in this way (through rituals). It is washed away by knowledge of God. (Adi Garnth 472)*

Perhaps the mention of cow dung requires explanation. The cow is a pure animal whose products are therefore purifying, hence the Hindu custom of using cow dung as a covering for the floor of the kitchen, the place in a house which must be most pure. Guru Nanak is saying that if the taking of life causes impurity, no one can be free from it if the argument is taken to its logical conclusion.

Bathing is the most common way of removing pollution. Of this practice Guru Nanak wrote:

> Should a man go to bathe at a place of pilgrimage with the mind of a crook and the body of a thief his exterior will, of course, be washed, but inwardly he will be twice as dirty as before. Outside he will be like a cleaned gourd while within he will contain pure poison. Saintly people are pure without such ablutions; the thief remains a thief even if he bathes in pilgrimage places. (AG 789)

His view on caste and social eminence is tersely summed up in these words:

> Caste is preposterous and worldly renown is vain. Only the One gives support to all. (AG 83)

He once spoke with caustic sarcasm of the white robed brahmin offering services for a fee at pilgrimage sites:

> Herons dressed in white feathers abide in places of pilgrimage. They tear and rend living beings and so are no longer white. (AG 729)

Of Islam's specialists in jurisprudence, Guru Nanak said:

> The qazi sits to administer justice. He tells his beads and mutters the name of God (Khuda or Quddus, the Holy One). He gives justice only if his palm is greased. (AG 952)

The hungry *mullah* he accused of turning his home into a mosque (AG 1245), to which the pious poor would come bringing donations.

It was not easy to be a Hindu or a Muslim, Guru Nanak warned, but he never said it was impossible. It meant taking God seriously and making the necessary social responses which were consequential upon it. It required the treading of the path of union with God:

> The way of union is the way of divine knowledge. With brahmins the way lies through the Vedas; the kshastrita's way is the way of bravery; the shudras way is that of serving others. The duty of all is to meditate upon the One. (AG 1353)

> *He alone is a brahmin who knows the Transcendent One, does deeds of penance, devotion, and self-restraint. He who observes the dharma of humility and contentment, thus breaking his bondage and becoming liberated, is a brahmin. Only such a brahmin deserves respect. He only is a kshatriya whose bravery lies in performing good deeds, whose body is yoked to charity and alms giving, and who sows the seeds of kindness. Such a kshatriya is acceptable in God's court. (AG 1411)*

In such passages Guru Nanak does not seem to be proclaiming a social revolution. The *shudra* should still serve others, but he does impose a similar requirement upon other classes. Humility, self-restraint, charity, and kindness all focus attention upon the other rather than oneself.

Similar verses can be quoted with reference to Islam. Two might suffice:

> *To be a Muslim is difficult. Only those who really are Muslims should be given the name. First, such a one should regard the religion of God's devotees as sweet and have effaced self-conceit as if with the file that scrapes a mirror. Becoming a true follower of the Prophet, let him put aside all thoughts of life and death. He should heartily submit to God's will, worship the Creator and efface self-conceit. Then, if he is merciful to all sentient beings, let him be called a Muslim. (AG 141)*

> *Make mercy your mosque, faith your prayer carpet, what is just and lawful your Qur'an, modesty your circumcision, and civility your fast. So shall you be a Muslim. Make right conduct your Ka'aba, truth your pir, and good deeds your kalima and prayers. (AG 140)*

Guru Nanak felt that it was not easy to be a Hindu or a Muslim. Ritualism which stressed the outward form of religious observance rather than the religion of the heart stood between the worshipper and God, and there was always the temptation to use religion, as he believed brahmins and teachers of yoga did, to dominate the credulous, or, as the mullahs and qazis did, to gain political approval from Muslim rulers.

Guru Nanak – mystic, social reformer, or political revolutionary?

Evidence for all these views can be found in the life and teachings of Guru Nanak, and from time to time each has appealed to Sikh and non-Sikh writers. Certainly he was a mystic if the term is used of someone who has direct inner experience of God. When nothing would deter Nanak from his vocation of serving God, his parents arranged his marriage. This was as ineffective as all other attempted remedies. The climax came one day when, aged about 30, he took his normal, daily bath in the local river, the Bein, and disappeared. Searches failed to discover him. Three days later, according to janam sakhi accounts, Guru Nanak returned to his village. In a hymn in the Guru Granth Sahib the Guru describes what had happened. He said:

> I was an out of work minstrel, God gave me employment. God gave me the order, 'Sing my praise night and day'. God summoned the minstrel to the divine court and bestowed on me the robe of honouring God and singing divine praises. (AG 150)

The imagery is that of a royal court where the king would appoint people to various posts and give them a robe of office.

It seems clear from such accounts as these that Guru Nanak was a mystic. However, in the early days of independent Indian, after 1947, Nehru condemned ascetics and recluses who seemed to contribute nothing to society. 'Aram haram hai' was his slogan; which might be translated as 'idleness is forbidden'. With this kind of 'mysticism' in mind, Sikhs have sometimes been suspicious when their founder is described as one. There are no stories of idleness associated with him; on the contrary Guru Nanak was a man of action. It would be wrong to suggest that he was a man who ignored the world through his devotion to God. He believed that God was present in the whole of creation, including all human beings. Consequently, he denounced aspects of society which, in his judgement, oppressed people and denied them their full humanity. He criticized the division of society into four varnas or classes because it denied the possibility of spiritual liberation in their present life to the fourth class, shudras, and to the so called untouchables who were outside it altogether. Into this group of spiritual rejects women also fell. Guru Nanak taught that there was one God and one humanity and that no one was beyond the reach of God's grace.

He asked those who considered women impure and incapable of spiritual liberation, *mukti*:

> *Why do you condemn woman, the one from whom great men and kings are born? It is through despised woman that we are conceived and born; it is to woman that we become engaged and married; woman is our lifelong companion who perpetuated the race.* (AG 473)

Unnecessary contact with Muslims was often frowned upon in the society in which Guru Nanak grew up. They were regarded as impure and carriers of spiritual pollution, as were Jains or the few Christians who might be encountered. Guru Nanak's companion throughout many of his journeys was a Muslim musician, Mardana of the *mirasi* or *dum* caste. His family, with its traditional occupation of singing and dancing at festivals and weddings, would have been regarded as low caste even after it had converted to Islam. By choosing the company of Mardana, Guru Nanak, a member of the twice-born *vaishya varna*, was making a statement about his attitude to class and the concept of pollution.

figure 3 Guru Nanak with his companions Mardana, holding the rebeck, and the HIndu, Bala, preaching to Bahi Lalo, a low caste carpenter, who became one of his followers. The Gurus are usually shown with haloes

Guru Nanak had no political power. Even at his death it is unlikely that the number of Sikhs ran to many thousands. However, this does not mean that political issues did not concern him. In 1520 the Mughal leader, Babur, sacked the town of Saidpur. Guru Nanak and Mardana not only witnessed the destruction, they were also taken prisoner. The janan sakhis describe a conversation that the Guru had with Babur who was a *sufi* mystic as well as a military leader. In it, the Guru interceded for the captives who had been taken by the Mughal army. As a result Babur released them. This incident hardly portrays Guru Nanak as a political revolutionary but it does demonstrate that the plight of the oppressed concerned him. So do the many passages in his hymns which accuse brahmins, *yogis* and mullahs of exploiting the credulity of simple people. It might be claimed that if the egalitarian teachings of Guru Nanak ever gained acceptance, the consequence for Punjab society would have been revolutionary.

Finally, there is a need to dismiss another interpretation of the purpose of Guru Nanak's word which some books still accept, though every scholar seems now to have rejected it. Sometimes it is said that Guru Nanak attempted to blend the best of Hinduism and Islam in a new religion that would appeal to both communities and bring them together. Hopefully, a moment's reflection will enable us to realize the inadequacy of the suggestion. Who is to define the 'best' of any religion, first of all? (Usually a Westerner using liberal Christianity as the criterion.) Secondly, there was no possibility of bringing together those who followed the teachings of the Vedas and the ministry of the brahmins, with those for whom the Qur'an was authoritative. It is, in fact, unlikely that he wished to create a religion at all, bearing in mind his comments on the inadequacy of religion!

In evaluating the role of Guru Nanak it is necessary to return to the words in which he described his calling. He said that he had been given the nectar of God's Name so that he could offer it to any who would drink it. Those who drank it would achieve peace and joy. He went on:

> *Your minstrel spreads your glory by singing your word. Through adoring the truth, Nanak says, we attain to the all-highest. (AG 150)*

Mysticism, social reform and political revolution might all be associated with Guru Nanak, yet he is best understood as none of these but as God's messenger or Guru to the Kal Yug, the age of darkness in which God's name and the spiritual liberation which it could give had been forgotten.

The word 'Sikh' means disciple. For many years it did not refer to men and women who belonged to a distinct religion but to people who followed the teaching that Guru Nanak and his nine successors gave.

03

initiation

Most permanent groups of people, political, social, or religious, devise some form of membership ritual. It may only be a membership card (after being nominated and upon paying the requisite fee) from the secretary, with a handshake being the only ritual act. It may be more elaborate, as when someone joins a uniformed organization and makes promises after passing various tests. The ceremony and the membership to which it leads gives coherence, identity and a degree of certainty to members – a feeling of belonging.

Sikh initiation is the only true rite of passage in the Sikh religion. It is an act of personal commitment. Ceremonies which will be examined later, such as naming and marriage, are not of the same kind either in terms of necessity or seriousness.

In the early days of Guru Nanak's preaching, a Sikh was merely a woman or man who responded to his message and became a learner or disciple of the path that he taught. Eventually, it came to have a more distinct meaning, especially when the Gurus began to wean their followers away from the beliefs and practices of Hinduism in particular. At some point, as happens commonly in guru cults, a form of initiation was introduced. Those who wished to become full members drank from a bowl of water that had been poured over the Guru's feet. They would commit themselves to a certain spiritual and moral discipline which would include rising early in the morning to recite prescribed hymns and meditating on others in the evening, earning a living by honest toil, and serving the community. Eventually, the time to change the form of initiation came, though the core of the spiritual and ethical discipline remained largely unaffected.

Vaisakhi 1699

At the Vaisakhi assembly of 1699 when the last Guru, Guru Gobind Singh, summoned Sikhs to join him at a town called Anandpur, the first Sikh initiation ceremony of the kind used today took place. The Guru had decided to stamp his unrivalled authority upon the Panth once and for all. Vaisakhi does not mark the transition of the Sikhs from a pacifist religious group to an armed community. There is no actual evidence that pacifism has ever been a Sikh teaching. In fact some Sikhs were already armed. Guru Hargobind had employed mercenaries and in 1609 had built a fort in Amritsar. From 1680 Guru Gobind

Singh was already training his followers in the use of arms. In that year he introduced a new rally which was called Hola Mohalla to coincide with the Hindu festival of Holi. This assembly was used to practise manoeuvres and for combat training. He had also fought battles and built fortresses, including the one called Keshgarh at Anandpur, to which the Sikhs were now summoned. Vaisakhi 1699 was the culmination of a process, the formalizing of existing practices. The main reason for the events of Vaisakhi 1699, however, seems to have been that the Guru had decided to confront and defeat the challenge of a powerful group, the *masands*. These were administrators used by the Gurus since the time of Guru Amar Das to look after the widespread Sikh Panth. One of their duties was the collection of offerings. Many, though not all, had become corrupt and some rivalled the Guru for control of the Sikh community.

Guru Gobind Singh dramatically called upon Sikhs to be willing to follow him, even to the point of death. He did so by asking them, sword in his hand, who would die for him. At first no one came forward, but eventually a Sikh volunteered and was led into a tent. The Guru emerged soon afterwards with what appeared to be blood on his sword. Four more times he issued his challenge and each time the same process happened until, after the last had been taken into the tent, all five Sikhs emerged alive with their Guru.

Conjecture often focuses upon what had actually happened to the five men. Speculation is futile and can be risky. To say that the Guru killed a goat, as has sometimes been suggested in books, is to upset vegetarian Sikhs of whom there are many. It also detracts from the main point, which is that the Guru was establishing his authority. With hindsight it can be seen that his action was also preparing his followers for the new situation of unrest and upheaval in Punjab that lay ahead after his death.

The Guru put water in a metal bowl, his wife, Mata Sahib Kaur, added crystallized sugar (*patashas*), and he mixed them with a two-edged sword and used the amrit (as this sweetened water is called) to initiate the five men who had offered their lives. They then initiated the Guru and his wife. Guru Gobind Singh then called for other Sikhs to come forward and receive initiation; many thousands did but some turned away, perhaps because they disapproved of force or were afraid, but mostly because it was clear that the Guru was creating a community in which any remaining considerations of caste and pollution had to be set aside. Initiates were going to receive amrit that had been prepared in part by a woman from one bowl and from the hands of men who came from a variety of *zats*. Daya Ram, the first Sikh to offer himself, was a kshatriya; Dharam Das was a Jat; Mukham Chand was an untouchable washerman; Himmat was a potter and Sahib Chand was a barber. At the point of initiation, those who came forward at Vaisakhi 1699 were confronted with their attitude to caste. Most brahmins, it is said, left the gathering.

The initiates were told that they were now members of a family, the Khalsa, which means the 'pure ones' and the 'Guru's own'. It was a term used by the Mughals to refer to land that was the personal possession of the sovereign, in the way that Sandringham and Balmoral belong to the British royal family and not to the nation as some other palaces do.

The first five Khalsa members were called the *panj piare*, the five beloved ones. Khalsa members were to wear five items of dress, which in Punjabi begin with the letter 'K' and are therefore known as the five Ks or *panj kakkar*. These are:

- *kesh*: uncut hair, including body hair. Regular washing should ensure that hair is clean, even waist-length head hair. Cleanliness is an important Sikh virtue. It should be remembered that all Sikhs should take a daily bath.
- *kangha*: comb that keeps the hair tidy.
- *kara*: a thin iron wristlet worn on the right forearm, though left-handed Sikhs have been known to wear it on their left arm. Occasionally, someone may be seen wearing a gold kara but this defeats the purpose of the five Ks, which are meant to be symbols not ornaments.
- kirpan: a sword with a single cutting edge. It might be over a metre long, as is the one carried by panj piare on all ceremonial occasions. Some Sikhs wear a very small one which is embedded in the kangha but many Sikhs disapprove of this and wear a short kirpan some 15 centimetres long. In Britain they will often wear it under a shirt or blouse on the left side of the body. This is done so as not to offend non-Sikhs who might regard it as an offensive weapon. The British government links it with the Scot's *skean dhu*. Guru Gobind Singh taught that the kirpan was a defensive weapon, to be drawn only as a last resort. Should you ask a Sikh to show you a drawn kirpan the request might well be met with a polite

refusal. As a friend said when I took some students to a gurdwara 'Sorry, Owen, but if it is drawn it should taste blood. You are my friend, I'm not going to stab you, and I'm too squeamish to prick my own finger!' Occasionally, there are fights in gurdwaras, as Sikhs must concede, and kirpans are sometimes used. If police are called, the law takes its course and Sikhs do not try to defend the actions of their members. The community is also likely to discipline such Sikhs. The kirpan should never be called a dagger, which is a weapon of deceit used by assassins!

- kaccha: short trousers or pants tied with a draw-string. In India and, possibly other hot countries, Sikh men may be seen working the land wearing a pair of kaccha. Elsewhere they are worn as an undergarment.
- Turban: men who are members of the Khalsa must also wear the turban as the Gurus did but it is not one of the five Ks. Women need not, it is sufficient for them to cover their heads with a scarf, but some women do wear a turban, especially the American 'gora' Sikhs mentioned on page 181. The purpose of the turban is not primarily to keep the hair tidy or free from dust, though it does fulfil this function. The kangha ensures tidiness, and bald Sikhs wear it, but unless you are living in a Sikh household you will not be aware of this, for the turban is put on immediately after bathing. With one exception, its colour and shape has no certain significance. Namdharis (see page 147) wear a white turban that lies flat across the forehead. Elderly Sikhs often wear white too, as do many young Sikhs who came to Britain from East Africa in the 1970s. The pattka, sometimes called a keshki, which Sikh sportsmen often wear, is no substitute for a turban. This should be clearly understood, especially by educationalists who do not like Sikh children wearing a turban in school. A child who has become an initiated Sikh, or who belongs to a family of initiated (amritdhari) Sikhs, must wear a turban as soon as he is able to tie one. This usually happens about the time of the tenth birthday. There is actually a turban-tying ceremony within the family to celebrate the event. It has led to a boy leaving school on Friday with his hair in a top knot (jura) and returning with the turban on the following Monday to the consternation of teachers! With better communication, such family events could be regarded as opportunities rather than threats. (Sikh families might welcome teachers to this, and to other domestic events.)

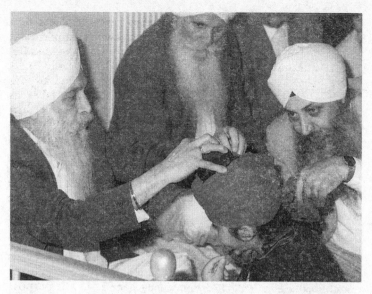

figure 4 the importance of the turban, even though it is not one of the five Ks, cannot be ignored by anyone who has seen a turban tying ceremony

The symbolism of the panj kakkar

The Khalsa symbols were primarily functional; the kaccha was more sensible for a warrior to wear than flowing robes or other similar garments of the period. The kara protected the sword arm and the kirpan was a popular weapon, easier to use than the heavier double-edged khanda. The uncut hair and the comb are less easy to explain in terms of practical usefulness. The kesh has always been regarded in the context of keeping the natural God-given human form, as opposed to Muslims who practise male circumcision, and Hindus who shave the head on certain occasions, or allow the hair to grow unkempt in the case of some groups of yogis. The hair with its comb indicates a disciplined spirituality.

Of the other Ks it is easiest and most convincing to find symbolic meaning in the kara. It reminds Sikhs that God is one. Sometimes they will say it is a handcuff that binds them to God. Frequently they will say that if they are tempted to do something wrong, as they put out their hand to do it the kara reminds them that they are Sikhs and God's people, their consciences are pricked and they refrain.

The kaccha are sometimes said to signify disciplined sexuality and the kirpan readiness to fight in the cause of the oppressed.

In the present day when the five Ks have, for the most part, lost practical meaning as a military uniform and weapons necessary for protection, it is natural to provide symbolic interpretations to justify their continuing importance and you may come across many meanings beside those mentioned here. They should be accepted with respect. In religion, authentic meaning is often that which the believer gives to something whether or not some scholar endorses it. Of course, the real justification for wearing the five Ks is the Khalsa member's obedience to the Guru's command.

Issues relating to wearing the 5Ks in public

Occasionally difficulties occur relating to the wearing of the 5Ks in public. Solutions *begin* with (a) understanding the Sikh position; (b) talking with elders of the Sikh community.

Kirpan Most have to do with wearing the kirpan in school where there may be a rule against carrying knives.

Amritdhari Sikhs must wear the kirpan and amritdhari parents may expect their children to keep the 5Ks. Most wear a kirpan about ten centimetres long under the shirt and trousers where it attracts no attention. Some will hand it over to the custody of the captain of a plane or the headteacher if requested to do so. Some will wear it as a symbol embedded in the comb (kangha). Some will agree to it being sown or riveted into its sheath so that it cannot be drawn but most would reject this solution.

The kirpan is not an offensive weapon and attempts should be made to persuade the workforce/school members to accept it as they would any other religious symbols.

Kaccha Sometimes pupils refuse to remove the kaccha to take a shower after PE. This situation has been resolved by them changing into another pair as they dry themselves.

Kara The free wristlet could harm another person during games or cause personal injury to a Sikh using machinery though the latter is unlikely. It may be possible to suggest that it be moved up the arm and held in place by elastoplast.

Turban This should no longer present any difficulty. The law clearly supports the right of Sikhs to wear turbans. However, occasionally Sikhs have suddenly appeared at work or school wearing one for the first time. It might be polite to warn people before hand, though why should this be necessary? Employers or headteachers should comply with the law.

Necklaces Sikhs may wear a necklace bearing a medallion of Guru Nanak. This is as much a religious symbol as a cross or a star of David and should be treated with equal respect.

In the end individual Sikhs will make their own decisions regardless of the advice of community leaders. That is Sikh egalitarianism.

The ethics of the Khalsa

More important is the requirement to keep a moral code, for it is not outward appearance that makes a Khalsa Sikh. Guru Gobind Singh commanded the new initiates to consider themselves children of the same parents, himself and his wife, with their home Keshgarh, the fortress at Anandpur where the original ceremony was conducted. Thus, all differences that existed prior to initiation were eliminated. They should pray daily, tithe themselves, and always keep the five Ks. They should never remove their hair, they should not eat meat from animals killed and prepared according to Muslim custom, they should not commit adultery, and they should never use tobacco or other drugs. Breach of any of these rules, called *kurahts*, would result in the wrongdoer becoming an apostate (*patit*). S/he could be readmitted to the order by repeating the initiation ceremony, but the sangat would first need to be assured that their penitence was sincere. In theory, a Sikh can repeat the amrit ceremony several times, but a second lapse is likely to be met by rejection of a third request. The patit can still attend the gurdwara and share karah parshad and langar. They will be told to be satisfied with that. Perhaps, some years later, should a lapsed member seem thoroughly repentant, s/he might be allowed initiation a third time. There are several minor prohibitions known as *tankhas*; breach of these requires an act of penance, not re-initiation. The penance, decided by the sangat might be community service – cleaning the shoes of worshipper in the gurdwara, cleaning the building, washing-up after langar . . . Interestingly, the penance should be practical – paying a fine would not do – and should not be humiliating, though it might be humbling. The aim is to reform the offender. Examples of tankhas are:

• dyeing the hair or plucking out white hairs!

- seeking a dowry for one's child as part of a marriage arrangement
- taking alcohol.

A new name

Members of the Khalsa took a new name. In the case of women it was 'Kaur', (princess), while men adopted the name 'Singh' (lion). Thus, Guru Gobind Rai became Guru Gobind Singh, and his wife Mata Sahib is known in history as Mata Sahib Kaur.

There were two reasons for the Guru's decision to adopt this method of naming. 'Rai' indicated that the Guru was a *khatri*. All family names inform other Sikhs of the *got* to which a person belongs. It is a constant reminder of the importance of caste and a potential source of discrimination because we learn a person's name first and draw conclusions before getting to know them at a personal level. 'Kaur' and 'Singh' were intended to nullify the influence of caste in the Khalsa. The Guru also told the Khalsa that they were now members of one family; one name endorsed this. By choosing Rajput names he was elevating them to the status of kshatriyas – warriors! Sikh names can confuse the unwary. For example, Teja Singh will identify a man as a Sikh and so will Teja Singh Dhillon, but they will not necessarily signify that he has been initiated. Only seeing the five Ks on his person will enable you to know that.

The amrit ceremony today

The tradition of 1699 is followed by Sikhs whenever someone takes amrit today. One difference is the emphasis upon maturity. In 1699 everyone who came forward was an adult, nowadays a request might be made for a whole family to be initiated together. The Rahit Maryada (the Khalsa Code of Discipline) stresses that age is not a consideration but that initiates should be mature enough to understand the implications of the vows that they take. This usually means that men and women, rather than teenagers, form the bulk of any group of people taking amrit, but I have seen it administered to a boy aged about ten, or even younger. Clearly the ceremony was little more than a formality; his mother wiped away the amrit with a towel to prevent it spoiling his suit! Sikh friends protested to me afterwards and condemned the whole proceeding. This was clearly an exception. More often than not one hears of Sikhs who are in their middle years or older taking amrit for the first time. They will say that they have deferred initiation until then because of the seriousness of the vows and their concern that they should be able to live up to the spiritual demands that being an amritdhari Sikh makes upon them.

Amrit pahul, *amritpan karna*, or *khande-da amrit*, which are Sikh names for the initiation ceremony, must take place in the presence of the Guru Granth Sahib. A copy will be taken to the room that has been prepared. It cannot be held in the main hall of the gurdwara during a service because public worship is open to anyone, including non-Sikhs, and at the amrit ceremony only amritdhari Sikhs and candidates for initiation may be present. Everyone will be wearing the five Ks. Seven people are needed to perform the ceremony – one to act as granthi, sitting behind the Guru Granth Sahib and five to be the panj piare. The seventh person is there as a guard to make sure that there are no interruptions. Of course, women as well as men may conduct amrit pahul. The people who are going to become Khalsa Sikhs are asked if they wish to be initiated. When they have made their affirmation of intent they are told what it means to be a member of the Khalsa by being reminded what Guru Gobind Singh told his followers in 1699. Then the ceremony begins.

The ceremony

The Guru Granth Sahib is opened at random and a passage is read out. Then comes the prayer, Ardas, after which the panj piare pour water into a steel bowl and keep adding sugar crystals to it. This is the amrit. They stir the liquid and recite some hymns at the same time. The hymns are:

- the Japji of Guru Nanak
- the Jap of Guru Gobind Singh
- ten verses (*swayyas*) by Guru Gobind Singh
- Chaupai, another collection of verses by Guru Gobind Singh
- six verses from the Anand, which was composed by Guru Amar Das.

These are hymns that Sikhs should use every day in meditation, so the panj piare and the initiates should know them well.

Here are a few verses from each of the passages used in amrit pahul.

> *When the hands, feet and body are covered with dust*

the dirt is removed by washing them with water. Filthy clothes can be washed clean with soap. But the mind that has been soiled by evil thoughts can only be made clean by loving God's Name. Virtue and vice are not mere words. We carry the effects of our deeds with us. Whatever seed is sown, the same fruit is reaped. Birth and death are decided by God. (Japji AG 4)

God has no marks or symbols, no colour or caste, no family line. No one can describe God's form, hue, features or attire. God is eternal, self-enlightened and of infinite power. (Jap, verse one, Dasam Granth)

Mighty elephants in gorgeous array, magnificently decked out in gold; thousands of horses nimbler than deer, swifter than the wind; their masters are powerful emperors before whom countless people bow. In the end such greatness crumbles to nothing as they go on their way. (Swayya 3)

God knows how everyone feels in their heart, what troubles good people and bad. From the ant to the elephant, we are all under God's kind eye. (Chaupai 11)

O my mind, concentrate on God, stick to God! Your sufferings will vanish. If God accepts you, you will succeed. God is almighty and can do anything for you, so why forget God? O my mind, keep fixed on God always. (Anand AG 917)

When the amrit is ready, some of it is poured into the cupped hands of each initiate for them to drink. This is done five times. Then it is sprinkled on their eyes and hair, again five times. Each time they say 'Vahiguru ji ka Khalsa, Vahiguru ji ki fateh!' 'Hail to the Khalsa, victory belongs to God'. If there is any amrit left, the initiates all drink it from the bowl. The final part of the service is the recitation of the Mul Mantra, and the giving of Sikh names to any converts. Then everyone in the room shares karah par shad from the same dish.

The meaning of initiation

A child brought up in a Sikh family according to the tenets of Sikhism is a Sikh. Initiation signifies a personal commitment to carry out all Sikh religious and social obligations in word and deed. Any sincere convert, regardless of background, may become a Sikh though Sikhism has ceased to become an overtly missionary religion.

Not all Sikhs are Khalsa members. As no central record of initiated Sikhs exist, and many gurdwaras do not even keep figures, it is impossible to say what proportion of Sikhs are amritdhari. Some sant groups (see page 186), some sangats and some families hold it to be of fundamental importance and therefore encourage members to take amrit, others give it far less priority, though Sikh writers and the Panth in general, one feels, stress it as the ideal to which all Sikhs should aspire.

Here may be the appropriate place to mention the names used to describe Sikhs who are not amritdhari.

- *Sahajdhari*. This is a Sikh who has not accepted initiation into the Khalsa for any of several reasons including, perhaps, disagreement with the Khalsa code. Such a Sikh will not keep the Rahit Maryada (the Khalsa code of discipline) fully. Sometimes the phrase 'slow-adopter' is used. This is incorrect and insensitive. There may well be no intention by the sahajdhari Sikh ever to become an 'adopter', i.e. be initiated.
- *Keshdhara*. A non-initiated Sikh who keeps the uncut hair and, inevitably, the turban.
- *Mona*. This term is sometimes used of a Sikh who is clean-shaven, cuts the hair and does not wear a turban. It would probably be unwise for non-Sikhs to use it.
- Patit. A lapsed Khalsa member.

Gurdwara management

Each gurdwara in the dispersion and many in India outside the control of the Shromani Gurdwara Parbandhak Committee or Delhi GPC (see page 154) is autonomous in terms of management unless it is a sant gurdwara. It may or may not have a constitution and elected committee. Those which do, usually have a rule that any registered member of the sangat may vote at elections but only keshdhari (and sometimes only amritdhari) Sikhs may stand for election. Not all gurdwaras allow women to serve on the committee, though usually they seem to have voting rights. Some years ago, in the 1970s, a gurdwara in middle England elected a committee entirely of women, save for one 'statutory male'! This was not so much to promote the cause of feminism as to show disapproval of the arguments and schisms within the sangat. At the end of the year they relented and gave control back to the men! Gurdwaras which exclude women from voting or serving on committees are going against Sikh principles.

04

the family

In this chapter you will learn:

- Sikhism is a family religion
- the nature of a Sikh family
- the extended family.

Sikhism is a family religion. This sentence can be understood in two ways. First, great emphasis is laid upon being a member of a human family. There is no place for celibacy and asceticism in the tradition. Secondly, it might be said that Sikhs regard themselves as one large extended family, at least ideally. In practice there may be tensions and disagreements but passages from the Guru Granth Sahib regularly remind Sikhs that humanity is one. Being part of that humanity, the Sikh community and individual families within it should also be united! The last Guru, Guru Gobind Singh, declared:

> The mandir (Hindu temple) and the mosque are the same, puja and namaaz are the same. Human beings are one, it is through error that they appear different.

> Their eyes are the same, their ears are the same, they are of one body, one build, a compound of earth, air, fire, and water. Allah and Abekh (a name used by some yogis) are the same, the Puranas and Qur'an are the same. All alike are the creation of the One. (Akal Ustat)

All the Gurus, with the exception of Guru Har Krishan who died at the age of eight, were married men. They affirmed positively the worth of family life and repudiated that of the hermit in such words as these:

> The One who created the world pervades it. Do not look for the True One far away. Recognise the Word (the Divine Spirit) dwelling in every heart. (AG 581)

There was no need, therefore, as ascetics did, to go to the forest in search of God. God could be found at home.

Guru Amar Das argued that the householder life was actually better than that of those who had renounced the world:

> Family life is superior to the ascetic life because it is from householders that ascetics meet their needs (i.e. by begging)! (AG 586)

But, of course, the householder life must be characterized by certain qualities. Guru Nanak said:

> He alone is a householder who checks his passions and begs from God meditation, hard work and self-restraint.
> The householder who gives all he can to the poor is as pure as the river Ganges. (AG 952)

Finding God in the home can be taken as referring spiritually to the teaching that God is immanent, within each human being. There is, therefore, no need to search elsewhere, but it is also understood by Sikhs to refer to family life. It is within the daily round of domestic life and responsibility that God is to be experienced. Hence passages in the Guru Granth Sahib which describe God as 'father and mother'.

The Hindu tradition speaks of four stages of life that a man passes through in journeying towards spiritual liberation – moksha. These are:

- student of vedic knowledge, *brahmacarya*.
- married family man, householder, *grihasthi* (Punjabi form).
- a third stage which might be described as that of retirement. The family business, if there is one, and responsibilities, will be handed over to the eldest son, and the father will give his time increasingly to religious pursuits, reading the scriptures, going on pilgrimage, meditating. This stage of *vanaprastha* should be entered when a man sees his son's son, that is when the family's future is secure and all domestic responsibilities have been met. His wife may share this stage with him.
- in the fourth stage of *sannyasin* all worldly attachments are laid aside. Wife and home are left behind, even the name that a man has used throughout his life is discarded. He may symbolically become dead to the world by cremating a clay effigy of himself as he passes into his new life of isolation save, perhaps, for listening to his guru's teaching. When he dies his body will be buried as he has no family to conduct the cremation rites. Not all Hindu men follow the path of the four stages or ashramas of life, especially the final one, but many do tend to see life as a progression in which the other worldly concerns of life are given increasing priority.

Sikhs reject the ashramas but retain this notion of progression. The Gurus taught that every Sikh should be a householder, grihastha. In this stage they should realize all the other stages.

As Guru Nanak taught:

> *Contemplation of the True One brings enlightenment which enables one to live detached even in the midst of life's hurly burly. Such is the greatness of the True Guru that through divine grace and guidance one can attain liberation even while surrounded by sons and wife. (AG 661)*

This is not to be understood as a sexist remark or to suggest that families can be a nuisance! It is a realistic recognition that the Indian peasant with many mouths to feed might find little time for spiritual development. The Guru is saying that it can be done and that the Sikh should not try to find excuses for deferring the cultivation of meditation and service, as well as the hard work which is a necessity, but which Sikhism makes into a virtue.

Consequently, once sons and daughters have completed their education, the family might begin to discuss their marriage. Undergraduates in their final year at college will frequently tell of family discussions and meetings being arranged with prospective partners. Among one group in Britain, the Bhatras (see page 184), it has become fairly customary for daughters to marry upon leaving school at 16. In this way, it is hoped that, by being kept within the close family circle, they will be protected from the kinds of relationships that many young people enter. The attempt has met with some measure of success but recently there have been divorces among young Bhatras as among other Sikhs.

Sikh marriages, in common with most marriages in India, including Christian, are usually arranged by the family. One reason for this is perfectly obvious. Friendships across the sexes are not part of Indian life. Attend a social gathering there, or among Indians who have settled abroad, and you will usually see the men and women sitting separately. Enter the canteen on a college campus and you will see male and female students at separate tables, unless a tutor is with them, almost as chaperone. In class, in gurdwaras, and in churches in rural areas, men and women do not sit together. If a tutor needs to converse with a student of the opposite sex it will be in a public area or the study door will be left open. Changes are taking place in Indian life and the pattern outlined above may be in process of being modified; you may, for example, see a young couple walking hand in hand in Delhi, but you are likely to be told that they are newly-weds who are expected to desist within a few weeks and immediately if, after the rarity of a middle class Western-style honeymoon, they are going back to the provinces! In a country where there is apparently not a word in its many languages to describe a friendship free from sexual content between man and woman, it is not surprising that marriages are arranged. Were it not so, in traditional society a couple would never meet and celibacy would be the rule!

The nature of family life is the other reason for arranged

marriages. The extended family or joint family is the norm in India. Someone once described a Hindu village with 600 inhabitants, as all being members of one family. It had its own temple, school, and medical facilities. Everyone belonged to the same occupational group. When a boy married it would be to a girl from a neighbouring village who belonged to the same occupational group. She would join him in the village. Girls, likewise, would marry men from other villages and go to live with their families.

When a family of grandparents, the sons and wives, their grandsons who may also be married, live together, perhaps under the same roof and sharing the same hearth and kitchen, it

figure 5 extended families may sometimes live together

usually, however, they will live in the same neighbourhood and meet regularly

note the paintings of Guru Nanak and Guru Gobind Singh which are to be found in most homes

is important that its members should be compatible to the greatest possible degree. Suppose a young man from a rural area went to agricultural college in Ludhiana and somehow met a medical student who, it may be adduced, came from a well-to-do urban family with its servants who did the cooking and cleaning. They fall in love and marry. She gives up her training, as would normally be expected, to live with her husband's family where she is expected to cook, clean, help on the farm and perhaps even lay a cow dung floor. This may be an extreme example but hopefully it demonstrates the importance of arranged marriages in an extended family culture and the sense of marrying within the occupational group. Even in a less contrasting situation a girl has to fit in with her mother-in-law who rules the kitchen, and existing and therefore senior sisters-in-law. Guru Nanak was well aware of the power of the bride's mother-in-law. He wrote:

> My mother-in-law is bad. She will not have me in the house. The vicious one will not let me meet my husband. (AG 355)

(The reference is presumably to those things that prevent the union of the soul with God, but the imagery used is one with which his audience would be fully familiar.)

Language often indicates where cultural strengths and weaknesses lie. In English there is nothing beyond the word 'cousin' other than derivatives such as second cousins, half cousin, cousin twice removed, and the like. A study of the Table of Affinity in *The Book of Common Prayer* reveals only eight words to cover 50 relationships. In Punjabi there are 50! And there are many more besides. There are two words, for example, for 'father's brother' depending on whether the brother referred to is younger or older than the father. Hierarchy in Indian families is very important and at a young age a child will learn the appropriate kinship terms and the conduct that is expected when dealing with the relative. Young girls will know that they can tease their sister's husband's younger brother but that they must be respectful to his older brother, if he has one. The husband, too, will know how to behave in different circumstances. In the presence of his older brother he will be expected to be deferential, even though he may be middle-aged. If, in a conversation with a third party, the younger brother seems to be monopolizing it, his older one will tell him in no uncertain tones to 'Shut up!' and sometime later may give him permission to re-enter the discussion.

One particular example of the precise meaning of kinship names might be given to demonstrate what has been described above. An aunt might be called:

masi if she is mother's sister
mami is she is mother's brother's wife
bua if she is father's sister
chachi is she is father's younger brother's wife
tai if she is father's elder brother's wife.

Children learn these names from an early age and acquire the behaviour proper to the relationship. 'Ji' is often added when more respect is being conveyed, for example, *'taiji'*. Sometimes, in Britain and other countries of the dispersion, these terms are not known and a child may talk about 'Portsmouth uncle' to distinguish him from another in Birmingham, but there are many second-generation Sikhs who do know the appropriate names and take a pride in such knowledge.

In traditional homes it is still customary for the men to sit down and be fed by the women, who will only eat when the men have finished their meal, especially if there are guests to be entertained. Daughters will serve the food the other women have cooked. If there are only sons the youngest of them will become an 'honorary daughter', if such a term can be used in an Indian context, and serve the men. Having said this, it must be added that there are households, not only Sikh, where the family sits down at table together and its male members take a hand in preparing the meal and clearing the dishes afterwards.

Domestic life being so hierarchical it is easy to realize how easy it is for a wife to be incompatible, not so much with her husband as with the family of which he is a part. The marriage of an agricultural student and his medical doctor trainee wife might only succeed if they were to set up their own home and establish a nuclear family. This would probably mean that the man would have to change his form of employment if his wife found an urban practice, or she might have to make sacrifices in a rural society and both might lose the security of their families, for the extended family, it must be noted, is a tremendously successful social security mechanism. For a vast number of people in India, there is no social support system. In their old age, parents depend on their sons to maintain them. That remains a reason for having large families and rejoicing at the birth of a boy more than a girl. A girl will marry and leave her home for another, probably accompanied by a considerable dowry. She is a liability from birth until her wedding day. In Punjabi she is described as being *paraya dhan*, the property of others. This explains, but does not justify female infanticide, still practised by some families, or bride deaths when a recently married girl is killed when the kerosene stove in the kitchen overturns and she is burned to death (the real reason being that the dowry was not paid in full, or the husband's family demands even more from her parents). The modern practice of amniocentesis to discover whether a child is female, and the use of abortion if it is, is only the latest method of restricting the female population. All these practices are in stark contradiction to the teachings of the Sikh Gurus. As long ago as the sixteenth century, Guru Amar Das said 'Cursed is he who kills a daughter' (AG 1413). The murder of anyone, as well as the use of dowries; is also specifically prohibited by the Sikh Code of Discipline.

Two stories may be told to illustrate the value of the extended family system. One is that of a friend preparing to go to India in the mid-1970s. He asked me to call on him the evening before his departure. Our conversation was interrupted by at least 20 family visitors, each bringing money. Some was the return of interest-free loans given a few years earlier to relatives who were setting themselves up in business or buying a house. (Borrowing from banks or taking out mortgages is something Asians prefer not to do. Moneylenders are the scourge of many rural families in India. The fact that Sikhs feel their treatment is related to the colour of their skin only serves to increase a natural reluctance.) Other contributions came from those who recognized their duty to assist a kinsman in need. In all he received about £2000 that evening. The second example is the story of seven brothers and two sisters. Their father had died. The eldest child found a job so that he could support the family and put his next brother through university education (there are few grants and scholarships in India). This completed, the second brother assumed the role of provider while his eldest brother went to college. Eventually the whole family of nine received an education, the girls were married, the older first, and then the brothers married in order of seniority. One of them took their mother into his home, of course.

The examples cited are Sikh but could belong to any Indian community. Arranged marriages are not of the essence of Sikhism. Love marriages can be equally Sikh, but foreign journalists and teachers who deplore the arranged marriage system ought to take the time to understand it before they encourage British children of Asian backgrounds to adopt Western ways. Often they are doing no more than exposing young people to life in a cultural no-man's land. Colour bars them from being fully accepted in one culture, the flaunting of family mores necessitates their father turning them out of the family if he is not to lose face among his kin and community, both in Britain and in India. Relatives still living there will not be slow to inform him that the chances of arranging marriages for their children are placed severely at risk because of stories reaching the village that he unable to control his own.

Pride (*izzat*) is very important in Punjabi culture. Family pride and its feared opposite, shame, play a great part in social behaviour. A family that has to call in social workers to help with a domestic crisis, a teenager running away from home, for example, will lose face in the community. Asian families are supposed to be capable of sorting out their difficulties without recourse to outside agencies.

Sikhs, as has been said, encapsulate all the stages of life in one, but when parents become grandparents they are likely to modify their behaviour and change their lifestyle. They will, of course, enjoy the company of their grandchildren and spend hours watching television, especially Indian films, but those who are devout will spend more time in the room of their house set aside for the Guru Granth Sahib, 'Babaji's room' as they call it, if there is one. If not, they may stay in their bedroom, for long periods reading their *gutkas*, books containing selected hymns, and meditating. The gurdwara becomes a place which they visit daily for many hours. There they can meditate and meet old people like themselves and reminisce about life in Punjab.

Because of the limitations of the English language in the area of relations, it is possible to hear a Sikh describing someone as his cousin-brother. This can be a way of distancing a relative. He may be near, but he is not close enough in respect to count as a full brother. 'Brother' is always used of someone who is a brother. It may also be used to describe someone who is highly regarded by the family, even though not a kinsman. It is a description to be valued and cherished. Cousin-brother is not!

Family ceremonies

There are three domestic ceremonies that Sikhs observe in a distinctive manner. These relate to the birth and naming of a child, marriage, and death and are examined in the next three chapters.

The proper behaviour of Sikh children

Asian culture describes a code of conduct for children that can still be found in Western Sikh communities.

Children should not offer their opinions in the presence of their elders or contradict them. Even if parents or other elders invite them to do so at some gathering, perhaps an inter-religious discussion involving young people, they may remain hesitant because the invitation is so unusual. They may also be anxious lest afterwards their parents are criticized by other members of the community who think they have been too forward!

'Look at me when I am speaking to you' is a usual request – or demand – when a teacher is reprimanding a pupil. Eye contact is a great form of rudeness in Asian society. Children and women should look down, not up! Personal decision making is not easily compatible with the extended family. A family in Punjab that owned a farm and several businesses decided that their son should become an accountant – why should other people know about their finances?

'Honour your parents' is a living Asian principle. It is not long ago that it was expected of children (and offspring remain children as long as parents and other elders live) that they should bow in front of grandparents and other senior members of the family and touch their feet. Muttha tekna may be less common in the West than in India and more a voluntary act of politeness and respect than a requirement, but the practice may still be found. It says much about the status of elders. (N.B. Sikhs touching the steps of the gurdwara and bowing before the Guru Granth Sahib are, of course, doing the same thing.

Cultures changes and the opposite of these situations can often be found, especially as most parents of Sikh school children living in Britain were probably born here, but they too have parents who may be severely critical of the way in which their grandchildren are being reared! (Not an exclusively Asian phenomenon.)

05

Sikh names and the naming ceremony

In this chapter you will learn:

- Sikh names
- the naming ceremony
- starting out in the Sikh community.

Parents seem to find many ways to determine names for their children. Some use family names, that of a grandparent, or one that has had a family connection over a number of generations. Others choose that of a popular film or pop star, always risky as someone years later may remember when Madonna was famous and work out the age of the person named after her! Some parents use name books which can be found in libraries or shops. Americans seem prone to keeping the same name over the generations and calling the new child John P. Smith the fourth. In past times, 'Septimus' and like names were popular among parents who seemed to be too exhausted to make other choices when number seven appeared!

With Sikh given names, one immediately runs into the difficulty that most of them can belong to men and women. So a letter signed Jaswant Sohel leaves you guessing whether to reply 'Dear Mr or Dear Mrs or Ms . . .' The Quaker way may actually be the simplest solution, use no title, simply 'Dear Jaswant Sohel', but even today that seems to be too familiar for some people.

Help may be to hand, however. The correspondent may have written 'Jaswant K. Sohel' as a signature. 'K' stands for 'Kaur' so you can be sure that you are dealing with a female.

But things are rarely as straightforward as they seem. Madanjit Singh is a woman who is trying to be helpful to the majority British or American population. Were she to use Madanjit Kaur when her birth certificate clearly showed her father to be Harbans Singh, it might cause legal problems. Indeed, until the late 1970s-80s, nurse Kaur was told that she must register as 'Singh', her father's surname, when she had qualified, otherwise she would not be put on the register. Those Sikh female nurses who complained were informed that if they did not like it they need not register and could begin the training process all over again. That situation has fortunately been remedied, and Sikh nurses may choose which name they wish to use for registration purposes. Apparently the French situation is not so simple. A Frenchman who converted to Sikhism wished to use the name given to him at his initiation. So far his attempt to become known legally by that forename has been refused and he has, for the moment, decided to spend no more money on legal fees.

In the West, a further complication may arise because most Europeans are unfamiliar with the naming customs of Sikhs, Muslims, Hindus and others. One day a young Sikh man was interviewed on television after rescuing some children from a blazing house. The caption described him as . . . Kaur! Enquiries in the community confirmed what you may have guessed: his mother 'Mrs Kaur', a widow, had been interviewed and, naturally, it was assumed that he, her son, must be called Kaur too.

A further concession to what often seems to be Western laziness is the acceptance of names used in the majority culture. People seem unable to cope with polysyllables so a young man named Charanjit calls himself 'John' and a young woman of the same given name is 'Sharon', even to her family. Sikh names are often given without any thought to their meaning and sometimes parents even make them up using their own given names. So Jaswant Kaur and Harminder Singh may call their child Jasminder, after all they say, s/he was the child of their mutual love, so what better than giving the baby a name compounded of theirs!

When addressing a Sikh, one may use Mrs Kaur or Mrs Singh. The full official Sikh nomenclature is 'Sardar Harbans Singh' or 'Sardani Baljit Kaur', but otherwise Harbans Singh or Baljit Kaur are acceptable. Harbans or Baljit on their own are not commonly used by Sikhs. Of course traditions change as people move from one culture to another, especially among younger people. Some wives may never call her husband by his given name in public, using instead, 'Mr Singh' or 'Mr Lal' for example. The daughter may answer the phone saying; 'This is Gurnam, dad isn't home yet', or, of her own husband; 'Paramjit is round at his mum's, can I take a message?' Younger couples now tend to use personal or even pet names in public.

Guru Gobind Singh introduced the names 'Kaur' and 'Singh' to replace the traditional family names such as Bedi, Sodhi, Sohel, Gill, Rathor, or in his case, Rai. From such family names, which represent the *got* (Hindi *gotra*) to which a person belongs, it is usually possible to discover their zat, (Hindi *jati*) and thus their place in the social hierarchy of India. Despite the advantage of the system, a glance at the Southall telephone directory with its many columns of Singhs, or reading an article by 'Harbans Singh' in a Sikh newspaper (there are at least six theologians or journalists who share the name, to my knowledge), the disadvantages can soon be recognized. Consequently, many Sikhs will use the got name. Sometimes one suspects that a certain element of family pride is also involved for while low caste people may use Singh to hide their got, those who come from the same got as Guru Nanak, a fairly high-ranking Khatri zat, are likely to be happily known as Avtar Singh Bedi!

Occasionally, a name may be common to more than one got, for example 'Birdi' also known as 'Verdi/Virdi' could be Ramgharia or Chamar. (The significance of caste in Sikhism will be discussed in Chapter 10.)

It should not have escaped notice that Guru Gobind Singh accidentally solved the surname problem that vexes a number of Western women nowadays. They do not wish to take their husband's name at marriage – so they keep their own, which is derived from their father! The use of 'Kaur' overcomes the difficulty completely.

Naming a Sikh child

Sikhs have their own special way of deciding what their baby should be called.

One couple, Harbans Kaur and Jaswant Singh, were thrilled when their baby girl was born. They lived in Birmingham and phoned relatives in India, Glasgow, Manchester and many other places. They also bought boxes of Indian sweets to give to neighbours and friends. Someone down the street who was not a Sikh and not familiar with Sikh ways was surprised when Jaswant Singh knocked on the door, gave him his news, and the sweets. At last, when he understood he agreed that it was a good custom. Harbans and Jaswant are modern Sikh parents, they value a daughter as much as a son, so they gave small presents to friends and relations. Some families only give presents if the baby is a boy, even though the Gurus said that men and women are equal and that girls and boys should be regarded as gifts of God. During the next few days relatives brought presents, specially at the weekend when people had no need to be at work. Harbans' parents brought clothes for their daughter and the baby, as well as turban lengths for their son-in-law. Other relatives gave money.

The birth of the child had also been marked by the following custom. A respected member of the community had visited the home, poured some water into a small metal bowl, added some honey and stirred it, while reciting the first five verses of Guru Nanak's Japji. A few drops of the sanctified water were poured into the baby's mouth, the rest was given to the mother.

figure 6 a baby given amrit during a naming ceremony

Sometimes, if this ceremony has not taken place in the home, the parents will take their baby to the gurdwara where s/he will be placed before the Guru Granth Sahib and then given some honey on the tip of a kirpan.

One Sunday, convenient to the family, the baby, already given the pet-name Rani (Queen) was taken to the gurdwara to be given a name. Harbans Kaur proudly carried the baby. Jaswant Singh brought some coverings, called rumalas, to put on the Guru Granth Sahib. The congregation sang:

I have the support of God, the almighty, so my sufferings and sorrows are over. Men and women alike, rejoice. God has been good to everyone. O devotees of God, there is peace all over because God's love has spread everywhere. (AG 628)

They also welcomed the new member of the sangat with this hymn:

God has been kind to me. The almighty one has fulfilled my longing. I have come home purified by

> *God's love and obtained blessing, happiness and peace. O saintly people, only God's Name can give us true liberty. Always remember God and keep doing good, day and night. (AG 621/622)*

As they sing this hymn the parents promise to bring up their child as a Sikh so that one day when she became an adult she could make her own personal commitment to God.

Another popular hymn is a verse that the mother of Guru Arjan composed when he was born:

> *Dear son, this is your mother's blessing. May God never be out of your mind even for a moment. Meditation on God should be your constant concern. It purges people from all faults. May God, the Guru, be kind to you. May you love the company of God's people. May God robe you with honour and may your food be the singing of God's praises. (AG 496)*

A member of the congregation stood facing the scripture and offered the congregational prayer, Ardas, then the granthi, who was a woman for this special occasion, asked Harbans Kaur and Jaswant Singh to bring forward their baby and lay her on the floor in front of the Guru Granth Sahib. She then opened the book at random and read the first new verse on the left-hand page. It began with the word 'Bishram' from page 818, so the granthi said the baby's name should begin with a 'B'. The rest of the family who were sitting near Harbans Kaur and Jaswant spoke quietly among themselves. Balwant, Baljit, Bakshish . . . why not Bishram itself, it meant peace. Harbans Kaur realized that if she chose it she would get some peace from the relatives who were pushing their favourite names! 'Bishram', she said. The granthi announced the name, 'Bishram Kaur' to the sangat and added loudly, 'Jo bole so nihal'. (A Sikh slogan of approval that cannot really be translated.) The congregation shouted back its agreement with 'Sat sri akal', the Sikh greeting which means 'God is truth'. Everyone shared karah parshad and friends gathered around the happy couple and the new member of the community.

Sikhs should consult the Guru Granth Sahib when naming each child in a family. However, it is possible to find families in which every child has a name beginning with the same initial, 'H' or 'G', for example. It is difficult to avoid the conclusion that the scripture was consulted once and the letter originally chosen was used on the three or four subsequent occasions. This, however, is not standard practice.

Naming converts

A convert to Sikhism would be expected to take amrit initiation and indeed would probably request it because it provides the clearest possible way of assuming Sikh identity. The naming ceremony described above will be incorporated into amrit pahul.

06
marriage (anand karaj)

In this chapter you will learn:

- the concept of marriage
- the wedding ceremony
- integrating into a new family.

A Sikh wedding service takes only 20 minutes to perform but the accompanying (strictly speaking non-Sikh and non-essential, but not unimportant) arrangements may take many months.

Even if the boy and girl have met and fallen in love at college or work and the parents have been persuaded to accept and endorse the relationship, the marriage is still regarded as the joining of two families. The letters, phone calls or journeys that might have occurred as kin attempted to find a suitable marriage partner would not now be necessary but there are still matters to discuss between the two families. No Sikhs who intend to remain in good standing with their families and their religion seem yet to have adopted the practice, described in some Victorian novels, of organizing a quiet wedding conducted by a compliant clergyman and witnessed only by a couple of discreet friends.

There may be a dowry to consider. True Sikhs fully obedient to the tenets of the faith should have nothing to do with demanding a dowry and some families let it be known that they will have nothing to do with the system. Many succumb and put themselves in debt to moneylenders for years to come, the victims of vanity and pride, concerned that their daughter will be well received by her new family. In the days before the wedding, the dowry and other presents will be displayed in the girl's home, together with the needlework that a village girl will have produced in her years of preparations for the great day of her life. The temptation for families to outdo one another on such an occasion can well be imagined.

Through meeting one another, the families can become acquainted. Often there is a tie of friendship somewhere behind the marriage – the couple may be the children of classmates or relatives of an uncle's wife for example, but tradition rules that marriages should not be within eight, or sometimes six gots. Put simply, if Gill and Dhillon are marrying, those names should not be found among grandparents or great grandparents. Nowadays, four gots are sometimes considered sufficient. Rules about gots are intended only to prevent the dangers that can arise from inbreeding. Otherwise they have no importance. The Rahit Maryada (see page 150) says Sikhs may marry anyone regardless of got. The only rule is that Sikh girls should only marry Sikhs and that child marriages are forbidden. The girl should be at least 18. It is usual for the groom to be older than the bride. Normally, marriages are between members of the same zat (caste), Jat marries Jat, Ramgharia marries Ramgharia, for example, (see page 185). Caste should have no place in Sikh marriages but in practice it is influential, though the number of inter-caste marriages is increasing and in America marriages with non-Sikhs are numerous, though not always accepted by all families.

In many countries a civil marriage is a legal requirement, with a religious ceremony optional, but England and Wales are examples of countries where a place of worship may be registered for the solemnizing of marriages. Some gurdwaras have become licensed; elsewhere the civil marriage is likely to take place in the groom's home town, followed days, weeks, or months later in the bride's gurdwara. As it is the religious wedding that matters to Sikhs, the civil wedding will not be accompanied by a lavish reception and only a few family members are likely to attend it. Bride and groom will return to their own homes and turn up at work next day as though nothing had happened, to the surprise of any non-Sikh friends who knew that they were getting married.

A Sikh wedding must take place in the presence of the Guru Granth Sahib and witnesses. This is really the only necessary requirement. In Britain this usually means that the gurdwara will be chosen. In India, in a different climate and where village gurdwaras are often small, a marquee might be used, even the crowded flat roof of a house with the overflow watching from other roofs. The groom would arrive on horseback followed by his male relatives and friends, perhaps with his youngest brother seated in front of him; sometimes this custom is still practised. In Britain, a nominal journey of a few hundred metres on horseback has been known. The sighting of hired buses or a fleet of cars, however, is the more normal way of heralding the approach of the groom's party.

Then the menfolk of each family will assemble for the ceremony of *milni* at which gifts are exchanged between equivalent ranking members. Men will usually give turban lengths or a shirt. The visitors will also be provided with refreshments. In Punjab, the tradition has been for only men to accompany the groom. The women stay at home preparing to receive the bride. Traditions, however, are changing and women relatives and friends often travel with men nowadays. There may even be a form of milni at which the women of the two families exchange gifts. This used to happen only when the groom took his bride, accompanied by her new female kin, back to her relatives for a visit some days after the wedding. When the groom arrives for the wedding he may also be mobbed by young women and girls of his bride's family who expect to receive presents. These preliminaries, however, are not necessary and vary as many wedding customs do, from one got to another though traditionally Sikh weddings are held before noon.

The wedding ceremony

The people attending the wedding will take their places in front of the Guru Granth Sahib, paying their respects to it first, of course. The groom, usually wearing a dark-red or pink turban, sits directly in front of the scripture. Eventually the bride with a companion, often a female relative, takes her place at his left side. The person conducting the ceremony asks the couple and their parents to stand as s/he leads the congregation in prayer invoking God's blessing on the occasion. An appropriate scripture passage is read and the couple are reminded of their duties to one another as husband and wife. They are asked if they will fulfil their responsibilities faithfully and when they nod assent, the end of the groom's scarf (*pulla*) is placed in the bride's right hand. They then stand to listen to the first verse of the wedding hymn, the *Lavan* which means encircling.

The four stanzas of Lavan, the wedding hymn composed by Guru Ram Das, read as follows:

> *By the first circling the Guru has shown the duties of the householder life. Sing the* bani *instead of the Vedas and hold fast to the faith which they reveal so that God may free you from all evil inclinations. Cling to righteousness and contemplate God's name which is the theme of all scriptures. Devote yourself to the True Guru and all evil will depart. Those minds are indeed blessed which are filled with the sweetness of the Name. To them bliss comes effortlessly.*

> *In the second circling you are to recognise that God has caused you to meet the True Guru who washes away the self-centredness of those who sing God's praises. I stand reverently face to face with the Guru. God is the soul of the universe, the only One, being within us and outside us. There is nothing which God does not pervade. Songs of rejoicing are heard in the company of the godly. Slave Nanak says, in the second round divine music is heard.*

figure 7 clockwise from the top left hand side of the page the illustration shows, the traditional dancing and singing with which women celebrate joyous occasions; putting mehndi on the bride's hand to symbolize happiness; the official meeting of the bride's and groom's families; the departure of the groom's party before the wedding, to the bride's home; traditionally his sisters feed the horse and plait its mane, now the party is more likely to travel by coach; and (centre), Lavan, the circling of the Guru Granth Sahib

*In the third circling longing for God and detachment
from the world wells up. By our good fortune, in
godly company, we encounter God whose purity is
found through singing divine praises. Good fortune
has brought us into the fellowship of the saints in
which the story of the ineffable One is told. God's
love fills our minds and absorbs us, as we have been
blessed with a good destiny which is recorded on our
foreheads. In the third circling, says Nanak, God's
love is awakened in the heart.*

*In the fourth round the mind attains divine
knowledge and union with God becomes complete.
This blissful state is reached through the Guru's grace.
The sweetness of the beloved pervades our souls and
bodies. God is dear to me and I to God on whom my
mind is fixed day and night. By exalting God I have
achieved my heart's desire. The beloved (God) has
completed the union. The bride's mind has blossomed
with the beloved's name. The beloved is united with
the holy bride. Says slave Nanak, in the fourth round
I have become one with the One.*

At the end of each verse the couple circle the scripture in a
clockwise direction, the groom leading, while the musicians sing
the stanza which has just been read. With the conclusion of the
fourth circling the couple are married. The prayer Ardas will
now be offered and will include a request for God's blessing
upon the newly married couple and their families.

Lavan uses the union of man and woman to describe the
relationship of God and devotee. Awe, love, restraint, and
harmony are the four steps outlined by its composer, Guru Ram
Das. They apply equally to the spiritual life as to the marital
relationship.

You might like to reflect upon what the marriage hymn tells us
about Sikh beliefs, note down a few points and reconsider them
when you have read Chapters 12 and 13 on Sikh theology.

After Lavan comes gifts, a coconut from the bride's mother,
coins and notes, some of which will be pinned to the groom's
shirt, while others join the coconut in the pulla. Bride and groom
will also be garlanded. Speeches and specially composed poems
and songs may be read or sung.

The reception

This varies from the fairly simple langar in the gurdwara to an elaborate buffet under a marquee in India, or in a hall in Britain, at which meat may be served, unless either family is vegetarian. At traditional weddings men will eat first (with non-Sikh female guests being given honorary male status). More often now, men and women mix together as families at the meal, the newly-weds sitting together.

Men have always danced *bhangra*, and women the female Punjabi equivalent, *gidda*, but not in the same place. Now, at sophisticated wedding receptions, there may be mixed discos with elderly bemused relatives watching and thinking how things have changed since their young days. Not, of course for the better!

Tradition is usually observed when it comes to the time for the bride to go to her husband's home. This ceremony called *sohli* is an occasion for mirth and grief. The bride will return to her parents' home to prepare for her departure. The groom and close male relatives will follow an hour or so later. They will join the family's menfolk in another room. The groom will sit with his wife and her relatives who will pester him and tease him until they receive presents; they are often given silver rings. The bride's mother blesses the couple. While his wife is preparing to leave, the new husband may be subjected to taunts in the form of jokes by her friends and relatives. They may comment on his clothes, his beard (if he is keshdhari) and his general physical appearance. He will be glad when his wife is ready to leave. She and all the womenfolk may wail, even if it is a love marriage, for she is leaving her family to enter a new one. The tradition of wailing, however, is condemned as not in keeping with the Sikh outlook on life, and is gradually dying out.

As the bride leaves home she is given a handful of rice to throw over her shoulder. This is a way of expressing a wish for the happiness of those who have come to see her departure. In India, this dohli ceremony takes place in time for the groom's party to be able to return to their village before nightfall but elsewhere, and if, for example, the couple are catching a plane for a honeymoon abroad, other considerations may affect timing. Traditionally, they would go direct to the husband's village, escorted by the men who had accompanied him in the morning. They would be given a mixture of water and milk to drink by the groom's mother when they reached his home. They would take seven sips from the jug and so would she. Inside the house the young people sit on the ground on a white sheet and are given a glass of milk to share. Then the groom leaves the room and his wife to be looked over and blessed by her new kinswomen. This can be a traumatic experience but she will hope that some of them remember the occasion when they joined the family, or will be thinking of the day when they will become part of a household of strangers, and will be kind and considerate to her.

A week later, or the next day sometimes in Britain, if there has been no honeymoon, the groom's family, including women, will take the bride back to her parents. Now a ladies milni will be held with its exchange of clothes, *shalwar-kameeze*, or maybe saris. The bride will be left for a week or so until, at a prearranged time, her husband returns and takes her to his family. Then their married life really begins.

Ties with the bride's family will not be severed completely. The story of the young Nanak going to stay with his sister Nanaki and her husband is but one example of many, but there is still a feeling among some parents that they should not be too demanding upon their son-in-law's hospitality. There is a custom of some women returning to their parents' home to have their first child, but this is not really a Sikh custom and does not seem normally to be observed in Britain, or elsewhere in the dispersion. There is also an understanding that couples may postpone having children for personal and career purposes, whereas in Punjab potential grandparents expect to have their craving satisfied within a year of the wedding. It is not unknown for a bride who is not pregnant on her first wedding anniversary to be sent home to her parents in disgrace and for a divorce to follow. This aspect of Punjabi or Indian culture should have no place among Sikhs who should acknowledge the gift of children as being in God's hands – and recognize that physically childlessness may be caused by men as well as women.

07

death

In this chapter you will learn:

- attitudes towards death
- the funeral service
- disposal of the dead.

Tender loving care is provided by the family, not the nursing staff in many Indian hospitals. They will camp in the grounds and stay with the patient through much of the day. They will prepare food at meal times. The professional nursing staff is there to provide the medical services which they have been trained to give. It has come as a surprise to Britons from the subcontinent to discover that sometimes strict rules for visiting hours are enforced, that a patient may only have two visitors at a time, and that s/he is expected to eat food prepared in the hospital canteen. Of course, members of the third- and fourth-generation are accustomed to this, having probably experienced it as children, or at the birth of a child. They may well be unaware of hospital regime in their ancestral homeland. For elderly people in the Asian communities, their first hospitalization can be a more than usually traumatic experience.

Should death be the end of the medical process, families expect to be with the person who is dying and to remain with the body for some time after death. To be removed while last attempts are made to maintain life, only to be informed that they have been unsuccessful and the loved one is dead, can make the family feel that they have failed in their duty. Sikhs should gather at the bedside to console themselves and the departing soul by reading verses from the scriptures, especially Sukhmani, the beautiful psalm of peace, to use the title given by many translators. It gives the assurance that anyone who meditated sincerely upon God's name will not suffer rebirth, but will live eternally with God.

Post mortems are greatly disliked by Sikhs. They seem to be a violation of the body of a loved one and they prevent funeral preparations being made. In India, the body would be cremated on the day of death, so long as the ceremony can be decorously performed before darkness falls.

Funeral rites

Death, when it comes, should not be an occasion for hopeless grief and loud wailing, though the lamentation that accompanies many Sikh funerals can be distressing to the outsider, especially a stiff upper lip Brit. Sikhs believe that death marks the transition from a life in which the knowledge and experience of God may sometimes be obscured by worldly cares and distractions, to one in which the joy of being in the presence of God eternally can be fully realized. As a line of the Guru Granth states:

The dawn of a new day is the herald of a sunset. Earth is not your permanent home. (AG 793)

The beautiful hymn Sohila which Sikhs should use in their evening devotions, sets out the aims of life as follows:

Know the real purpose of being here, gather up treasure under the True Guru's guidance. Make your mind God's home. If God abides with you undisturbed, you will not be reborn (AG 13)

The evidence for a life beyond the present one lies for the Sikh in such assurances as these, in the belief that the Gurus themselves were living in the divine presence when they were commanded to resume a human form to preach God's message to humanity, and in personal experience. Some people become *jivan mukt*, that is they attain liberation while still in their human bodies. This would be considered the logical conclusion of the Gurus' emphasis upon God as immanent. Sikhs would speak of a relationship with God that they could not envisage as ending at physical death. God's love is eternal.

Funeral services should proclaim the hope and promise of eternal life. Sorrow is natural but the mourners should be reminded of the fuller life that the departed now enjoys.

Sikhs tend to prepare the body themselves and dress it in the five Ks. This is done in many areas of the dispersion by arrangement

figure 8 Sikhs usually act as pall bearers at funerals and carry out as many of the cremation ceremonies as possible themselves. It is the last opportunity to show respect

with a firm of undertakers who have become accustomed over the years to conducting Sikh funerals. As previously mentioned, the custom in India is to cremate the body on the day of death, unless the time of death was too late for the ceremony to be carried out before evening which, even in summer, is no later than 5.00 p.m. In Britain the funeral should take place as soon as possible after death.

In rural Punjab 'Vahiguru Sat Nam' will be repeated and hymns will be sung as the procession walks to the cremation ground. In the West, these are chanted at home and in the gurdwaras by the congregation. The coffin will remain open so that last respects may be paid. The Sikh Code of Conduct lays down the order of service, which should therefore be the same in general terms throughout the world:

> *The dead body is washed and clothed (complete with the five symbols) before it is taken out on a bier to the cremation ground. The procession starts after a prayer and sings suitable hymns from the Guru Granth Sahib on the way. At the cremation ground the body is placed on the pyre, the Ardas is recited, and the nearest relatives light the pyre. When the pyre is fully ablaze, someone reads Sohila and offers prayers for the benefit of the dead. Then the people come away, and leave the relatives of the deceased at their door, where they are thanked before departing (pages 17–18)*

In Britain and elsewhere where there are public crematoria, the essentials of this instruction are observed though a hearse and private cars, or hired buses are used. Male relatives will formally help to put the coffin in the incinerator.

After the funeral Sikhs may return to the gurdwara.

Disposal of the dead

Guru Nanak was asked whether the Hindu custom of cremation or the Islamic method, inhumation, was the correct one. He refused to enter into the controversy but did humorously point out that the best clay for making pots seemed to be found in cemeteries, so there was a chance that the decomposed body ended up by being burned! (AG 466). There is a continuing argument among his followers as the story is told that when the

Guru was dying those who came from a Hindu background asked for permission to cremate him; the Muslim devotees wished to bury him. Guru Nanak told them to cover his body with a cloth and place flowers by it, Hindus one side and Muslims the other. Those whose flowers remained fresh may dispose of the corpse as they wished. In the morning they found both groups of flowers still fresh, but the body had gone! The Guru was indifferent to how the body should be dealt with. The only thing that mattered was the state of the soul. If it had not achieved liberation, its prospects were bleak indeed. In fact, Sikhs today tend to accept the custom of the land in which they live. For choice they cremate but in Arab countries where this is not possible they may bury their dead, though some may fly the body back to Punjab.

British Sikhs sometimes arrange for the ashes of their dead relatives to be taken out to sea and thrown into the water while prayers are said. Leeds Sikhs are an example of a community who have asked for a riverside platform to be erected from which ashes can be cast into a local river. This has met with opposition from environmental groups and local residents who fear, among other things, large numbers of Sikhs gathering for the deposition ceremony. These anxieties are understandable but are not grounded in fact. Sikhs may gather in their hundreds at the crematorium but, in common with the tradition in many other religions, only a few close relatives are likely to be present to scatter the ashes. The issue of river pollution may be real but authorities must be careful to be sure that objections are not really based on dislike of something new, and therefore strange.

Despite their dislike of post mortems, Sikhs do not object on principle to the use of organs from dead people to improve the quality of life of the living. Of course, as in all religions, bereaved relatives may refuse because they find the notion of the body of a loved one being mutilated distasteful.

The Code of Discipline forbids 'the erection of monuments over the remains of the dead' (p. 17). This is because of the Hindu and Indian Muslim custom of making the burial place of a saintly person a focus of devotion. The sangat can give spiritual as well as physical comfort and moral support. Samadhis, resting places for the remains of devout men and women, encourage practices which Sikhs regard as superstitious.

08

the Sikh Gurus

In this chapter you will learn:

- the ten human Gurus
- the concept of Guru
- respect for the Gurus.

We have already studied the life of Guru Nanak in examining the beginnings of the Sikh religion. He was the first of ten Gurus. Now is the time to consider their contributions to the development of Sikhism.

The list of the ten Sikh Gurus is as follows.

Guru Nanak,	15 April 1469,	died 1539
Guru Angad,	31 March 1504,	Guru 1539–52
Guru Amar Das,	5 May 1479,	Guru 1552–74
Guru Ram Das,	24 September 1534,	Guru 1574–81
Guru Arjan,	15 April 1563,	Guru 1581–1606
Guru Hargobind	14 June 1595,	Guru 1606–44
Guru Har Rai,	30 January 1630,	Guru 1644–61
Guru Har Krishan,	7 July 1656,	Guru 1661–4
Guru Tegh Bahadur,	1 April 1621,	Guru 1664–75
Guru Gobind Singh,	22 December 1666,	Guru 1675–1708

Birth dates are given because these are often celebrated as festivals, especially in their place of birth. Only the deaths of the two martyr Gurus (Arjan and Tegh Bahadur) are similarly commemorated, but now they are usually observed according to the lunar calendar and therefore the Gregorian date varies from year to year. Guru Nanak's birthday is celebrated in November, following a longstanding tradition which accepted his birthday as occurring on full moon day in the month Kartik (November).

Guru Nanak began his ministry in about 1499; Guru Gobind Singh ended his in 1708 when he conferred gurasling upon the scripture. The Sikh story is very much that of the achievements of these ten men. It is tempting to ask which of them was the most important but at this point it is necessary to bear in mind a Sikh teaching summed up in a verse from the bards Satta and Balwant who sang at Guru Arjan's court. They said:

The divine light is the same. The life form is the same (i.e. human).
The King has merely changed his body. (AG 966)

In other words, all the Gurus shared the same ministry, manifested the same teaching and were therefore equal. Sikhs see no difference, for example, between the criticism which Guru Nanak made of the Mughal Emperor Babur's injustices when he sacked Saidpur, and the militant opposition of Guru Gobind Singh to what he saw as the oppressive regime of the Emperor Aurangzeb 200 years later. The principle of opposition to injustice is the same.

Guru Nanak

Guru Nanak was the first Guru and, as the words of Satta and Balwant indicate, the human source of the teachings of Sikhism. Sikh doctrine is essentially that taught by Guru Nanak. Also, such things as congregational worship and the custom of eating together (langar) can be traced to him. Before he died, Guru Nanak appointed a successor, Guru Angad. Satta and Balwant state that when he had installed him, Guru Nanak bowed to him. From this one might argue that Guru Nanak regarded Guru Angad as more important than himself. However, what they actually say is:

> During his lifetime Guru Nanak made obeisance to his disciple. (AG 966)

By this act, Guru Nanak was publicly affirming the guruship of Guru Angad in the presence of men and women who might have considered supporting one of his two sons.

Guru Angad

Guru Angad finalized the gurmukhi script in which the Guru Granth Sahib is written, collected the hymns of Guru Nanak, and managed to ward off the challenge of the Guru's son, Shri Chand, who felt that he should have succeeded him as leader of the Sikhs. The second Guru was a consolidator rather than an innovator, but the Panth may well have needed that kind of leadership after Guru Nanak's death. Even though he only wrote 62 hymns, his place within Sikhism is significant.

Guru Amar Das

Guru Amar Das was faced with a growing and widespread Panth. If groups of Sikhs were to be found in most of Punjab, we have to imagine him being responsible for the spiritual development of people living in a region as large as England, in days when there was no public transport and the Mughals were only beginning to develop the important Grand Trunk road from Kabul to Calcutta, via Delhi. He divided the area where Sikhs lived into 22 *manjis* or regional groups, each one led by a *sangatia*. He appointed women preachers, an important step in a Muslim-influenced society where women might not have been permitted to have contact with men outside membership of the family. He maintained Guru Nanak's social justice concern, persuading the Emperor Akbar (1556–1605) to repeal taxes on pilgrims going to the holy site of Hardwar on the river Ganges. On one occasion, Emperor Akbar visited the Guru who made him sit in line with those who were taking food from the Guru's free kitchen (langar), before discussing religious matters with him. In doing so he introduced the principle of 'Pehle pangat, piche sangat', 'First eat together and then worship together'. By emphasizing the importance of commensality, introduced by Guru Nanak, Guru Amar Das was striking a practical blow against the belief that a person should not take food with someone of a lower caste, women, or members of another religion. The Guru also established a *baoli*, a place for ritual bathing, at Goindwal where he lived. This became an alternative to Hardwar as a place where Sikhs went for ritual cleansing. Although the Gurus frowned on such practices and the beliefs which underlay them, it is possible that complete families were now joining the Panth rather than enthusiastic and convinced individuals, and Guru Amar Das realized that they could not be easily weaned away from beliefs in sacred places; therefore, he decided instead to deflect their attention from Hindu sites to one that was Sikh. The practice of requiring all Sikhs who were able to gather in the Guru's personal presence at Vaisakhi and Divali, important Hindu festival times, was another way in which he encouraged the development of a distinct Sikh identity. The problem of the nominal believer seems to begin with the second generation of converts who sometimes lack the conviction of the first converts. This may have been Guru Amar Das's way of responding to the situation.

Guru Ram Das

Guru Ram Das built the town of Ramdaspur, which later became Amritsar, the focus of Sikh religious life. This was the beginning of a policy of urban development which his son continued. He, too, was a social reformer, denouncing the practices of *sati*, the immolation of women on their husband's funeral pyre, and the veiling of women. Widow remarriage was encouraged, should the woman so desire. Presumably, Muslim culture was becoming more influential in Punjab and he was eager to combat some aspects of it which he considered harmful, such as the seclusion of women. Like the earlier Gurus, he composed hymns, the most famous of which was the Lavan, to be used at all weddings (see page 65).

Guru Arjan

Guru Arjan inherited a Panth which was large, widespread in Punjab, and wealthy. He strengthened it by continuing the urban program of his father, building the towns of Taran Taran, Shri Hargobindpur, (named after his son), Kartarpur (named after the village established by Guru Nanak, but on a different site), as well as completing the town of Amritsar. It was there that he built the Darbar Sahib, the complex focused on the Harimandir Sahib, the gurdwara that was given the name Golden Temple by the British. More important, he collected the hymns that Sikhs used in their worship and put them together in one authoritative collection, the Adi Granth, which he installed in the Harimandir Sahib in 1604. This attracted the attention and approval of Akbar who was ecumenical in his religious interests, so much so that his more orthodox Muslim advisers feared that he might convert to another religion, though in fact he was a devout Muslim. It may be that Guru Arjan hoped that the growing Panth might provide the solution to India's religious division. If any Guru ever saw Sikhism as the religion of reconciliation, it must have been Guru Arjan. After his period of leadership, the opportunity never recurred. In fact, it came to an end, literally, with his death. In 1605 Akbar died. His successor, Jehangir, accused Guru Arjan of supporting a rival contender for the Mughal throne. He was arrested and put to death in Lahore. Sikhs regard him as their first martyr.

Guru Hargobind, Guru Har Rai and Guru Har Krishan

The next three Gurus made less of a contribution to the development of the Panth than the five who came before them. Guru Hargobind responded to the changed times which led to his father's death by maintaining a standing army of mercenaries and symbolically wearing two swords, one representing spiritual power, *piri*, and the other temporal power, *miri*.

The seventh Guru, Har Rai, defended the integrity of the Adi Granth. The emperor of his day, Aurangzeb, had been told that it was disrespectful of Islam. The Guru sent his son, Ram Rai, with a copy of the scripture to the Mughal court. Faced with criticism, Ram Rai was willing to modify some words in the Adi Granth. The Guru repudiated him and Ram Rai became the focus of a rival movement supported by the court.

Guru Har Krishan was only five years old when he became Guru. He died of smallpox at the age of eight. Nevertheless, he is remembered in the Sikh congregational prayer, Ardas, as the one whose 'sight dispels all pain' because during the plague he cared for sufferers until he became ill himself.

Guru Tegh Bahadur

The ninth Guru, Tegh Bahadur, rallied his community and supported Hindus in resistance to Aurangzeb's policy of Islamization. He was eventually captured and executed in Delhi, becoming the second martyr Guru. Like the first five Gurus, he composed hymns.

Guru Gobind Singh

His nine year old son became the last Guru in 1675. Guru Gobind Singh is remembered for two major decisions. The first was to create within the Sikh community, the Khalsa, Sikhs who took special vows of loyalty including readiness to use arms in righteous cause. The Khalsa was formed in 1699 and the outward appearance of the Sikh, the five Ks and the turban (in the case of men), dates from this time. In 1708, just before he died, the Guru conferred guruship on the scripture, now known as the Guru Granth Sahib.

Sikh attitudes to the Gurus

This can be summed up in one brief statement; profound respect falling well short of worship. The Gurus themselves were emphatic in admonishing their followers against regarding them as *avatars*, divine incarnations. To view a guru as divine is natural within the Hindu context. Each human being is indwelt by the *atman* which is pure spirit and, according to some teachings, separated from the Absolute (Brahman) only by ignorance. When that ignorance is removed the union of atman and Brahman becomes realized. A guru is one who has achieved this and so passes beyond the human condition of being motivated by such things as desire or anxiety. When Guru Arjan said:

> *May the mouth burn which says that God becomes incarnate, God neither comes to nor departs from this*

earth. The God of Nanak is all-absorbing and ever present. (AG 1136)

and Guru Gobind Singh reaffirmed it with equal forcefulness:

Those who call me Supreme Being shall fall into the pit of hell.
Recognise me only as God's servant; have no doubt about it. I am the slave of the Supreme Being.

Some of their audiences must have been confused because Gurus often asserted their union with the one. The Sikh Gurus, however, were requiring their followers to look beyond them to the divinely revealed Word which they uttered and to the One from whom it came and who was immanent in each of them. An

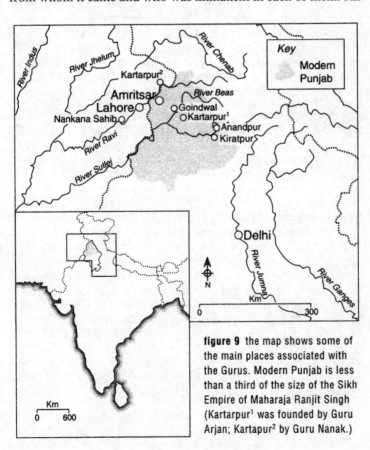

figure 9 the map shows some of the main places associated with the Gurus. Modern Punjab is less than a third of the size of the Sikh Empire of Maharaja Ranjit Singh (Kartarpur[1] was founded by Guru Arjan; Kartapur[2] by Guru Nanak.)

essential part of their message is that there is no distinction between Guru and disciple:

The Guru is the disciple and the disciple is the Guru.

This having been said, it is important to recognize that Sikhs regard the Gurus with great reverence. Their actions are not a subject for criticism, being divinely inspired. Iconographically, pictures often show them with haloes and of paler complexion than any other people who may be depicted. Under the picture may be written the words 'Guru Nanak Dev Ji' or 'Guru Gobind Singh Dev Ji'. The honorific title 'Dev Ji' is to be found under similar pictures of Hindu deities. However, it is not usual to find such pictures garlanded, and similar ones of Krishna or Durga might be in Hindu homes or temples, and Sikhs never bow toward pictures of the Gurus. In gurdwaras, portraits of the Gurus should be kept well away from the Guru Granth Sahib so that no confusion may arise in the mind of young or uneducated Sikhs. In some gurdwaras, no such pictures are to be found in the worship room so that nothing might even appear to rival the authority of the Guru Granth Sahib.

Sikhs would prefer their Gurus not to be represented as characters in a drama, though words attributed to them might be spoken in the third person in some kind of tableau of the story of the first amrit ceremony (see Chapter 03). In such situations, most likely to occur in school and in an area where Sikhs live, it is always advisable to discuss any proposal for celebrating Vaisakhi or Guru Nanak's birthday with members of the community. They are likely not only to provide the kind of advice that avoids embarrassment but also to give generous help towards making the event successful and memorable. There is often considerable good will in the community towards those who demonstrate a respectful concern for the teachings of Sikhism, and the welfare of Sikh children. Harm is usually done by thoughtlessly failing to recognize that groups such as Sikhs have other attitudes to those of us brought up with a somewhat secular outlook, even Christians. This comes out most clearly in the respectful treatment of the Guru Granth Sahib (see page 119), but it can also take the form of an Open University student placing a copy of a book in Sikhism bearing a picture of Guru Nanak in the shoe rack of the gurdwara and putting her shoes on it, or the carelessness of an author failing the capitalize the 'G' in the name of a Sikh Guru.

The human Gurus differ from other people in the nature of their birth. Karma explains the birth of most people. Human birth is the consequence of past deeds. Not so with the Gurus. Sikhs believe that they were already liberated beings, living in the divine presence, when they were commanded to take human form again in order to bring knowledge of God to an age which no longer knew the path of spiritual liberation.

In his poem, *Vachaitar Natak*, Guru Gobind Singh wrote:

> *When God gave me the order. I assumed birth in the kalyug, I did not desire to come as my attention was focused on God's feet. God remonstrated with me and sent me into the world.*

> *(quoted in Macauliffe vol. V. p. 296)*

Here we are apparently presented with something which at the least appears to be very close to the Hindu concept of *avatar*. In earlier verses of the poem he has even traced his descent to Rama and beyond him to the king Raghu and Kesain (Kalsain), the sage of the Vedas (Macauliffe, p. 290-1). However, the purpose of the Guru's birth is to proclaim Nam, to call men and women to the worship of the One God which had been neglected and forgotten, even though God had sent many messengers. The list catalogued by Guru Gobind Singh included Vishnu and Brahma, Mahadev (Siva), Goraknath, Ramanand, and ended with Muhammad, of whom he wrote:

> *I then created Muhammad, king of Arabia. He too established a religion of his own, cut off the foreskins of his followers, and made everyone repeat his name.*

He ends his comments upon these messengers by denouncing them all, in words attributed to God, for attempting to turn people to themselves not to the one who sent them.

> *No one fixed the True Name in man's heart. All these were wrapped up in themselves and none of them has recognised me, the Supreme Being.*

God continues:

> *I have glorified you as my son, I have created you to proclaim the Panth. Go spread the faith there and restrain the people from senseless acts (p. 299).*

To this the Guru responded:

> *I stood up, clasped my hands, bowed my head, and replied: 'Thy religion shall prevail in the world when thou providest assistance.'*

He then explains his birth and his relationship to God:

> For this reason the Lord sent me. Then I took birth in
> the world. What he spoke, that I speak, and I bear no
> enmity against anyone.
> Those who call me Supreme Being
> shall all fall into the pit of Hell. Recognise me as
> God's servant only: have no doubt of this. I am the
> slave of the Supreme Being (p. 299/300).

Both Guru Nanak and Guru Gobind Singh explicitly stated that
they were rare, extraordinary human beings in the sense that
their birth was the result of God's will (hukam), not previous
karma. They belonged to the category of human beings who had
achieved liberation, but had returned to earth at God's bidding.
In the words of Guru Arjan:

> Above birth and death are your holy ones, for they
> come into the world to do good to others. They bless
> all with gift of spiritual life, lead all to your worship
> and unite all with you. (AG 749)

Some non-Sikhs have interpreted the poem literally but Sikh
commentators would see an element of poetic hyperbole in Guru
Gobind Singh's poem: the words of a leader wishing to inspire
his people, rather than express a theological statement. They
would certainly draw attention to the part of Vachitar Natak
which was quoted at the beginning of this section in which the
Guru denounced anyone who equated him with God.

Indian gurdwaras to visit

Anyone who can should visit the Harimandir Sahib in Amritsar
during the day and for Sukhasan and Parkash karna if possible
(see p.119).

Three important gurdwaras to visit in Delhi are:

Bangla Sahib on the site where Guru Har Krishan died;

Sis Ganj in the old city at the place where Guru Tegh Bahadur was
executed;

Rekab Ganj where the body of Guru Tegh Bahadur was cremated.

The stories connected with these and other gurdwaras are in *Sikh
Shrines in India* by G S Randhir listed in Taking it Further, page 193.

09

festivals and their meaning

In this chapter you will learn:

- information about the major festivals
- the Sikh calendar
- Gurpurbs and melas.

Sikhs treat all days in much the same way so for the outsider, especially in the West, it may be difficult to get a feeling that their festivals are particularly important unless you are in one of the main centres where a celebration is taking place. They have no weekly holy day and shun any idea of auspicious days and are therefore totally at ease in observing a festival on the weekend following its actual date. There has usually been no tendency to keep children away from school on the holy day in Britain, though Sikh schools in India may close or organize special celebrations, as also do the voluntary aided schools in England.

This attitude is likely to continue unless external pressures prompt (or perhaps provoke) Sikhs to behave differently. If, for example, other religions demand holidays so that they can observe certain occasions local Sikhs might follow suit so as not to be outdone.

Sikhs have recently introduced a calendar dating from the birth of Guru Nanak in 1469. It is called the Nanakshahi Calendar and counts the birth year of Guru Nanak as year one. In Guru Nanak's India the calendar was based on the Bikrami/Vikrami or Samvat era, which began in the year 58 of the Gregorian calendar. Thus the Janam Sakhis say that Guru Nanak was born in Samvat 1526 (1468/9 CE). Early Sikh writings, in the days before European influence, naturally used the Samvat system and a few modern books retain it still as their authors attempt to distance themselves from the Raj!

The first use of festivals by Sikhs came in the time of Guru Amar Das who commanded his followers to assemble in his presence on the Hindu spring and autumn festivals or melas meaning fairs, of Vaisakhi and Divali and Hola Mohalla. This was clearly a way of implementing his policy of developing a distinctive Sikh identity. People, at these times, had to choose where they belonged, with their Hindu kin or with the Guru. Festivals are important in forging and expressing identity, as some of the comments made above have implied and this is what Guru Amar Das successfully did. The Sikh melas combine religious purpose and sheer festive enjoyment in the main places where they are observed.

figure 10 the illustration is designed to show that Vaisakhi brings tgether the historic events of 1699 and present day celebration. It is common for initiations into the Khalsa to happen at this time. Clockwise from top left Mata Sahib Kaur and Guru Gobind Singh preparing the first amrit; Keshgarh Sahib gurdwara on the site where the first amrit ceremony was held; two Sikh children wearing the five Ks; a modern amrit ceremony; and, centre, a Vaisakhi procession led by the panj piare

figure 11 Guru Hargobind is best known among Sikhs for his freeing of 52 rajas. At Divali the Darbar Sahib is illumined to commemorate the event

Gurpurbs

The majority of Sikh festivals are gurpurbs, anniversaries of Gurus' birthdays and occasionally deaths, plus the anniversary of the first installation of the Adi Granth. Sikhs celebrate them in the same way wherever they live. The main activity is a continuous reading of the Guru Granth Sahib, an akhand path, which is timed to take 48 hours and ends on the morning of the day when the *gurpurb* is being observed, usually a Sunday. (Occasionally, a gurdwara may keep the birthday of Guru Nanak in the very early morning as tradition records that he was born at that time on a moonlight night during the fragrant hour which is the last watch of the night (i.e. the hours before dawn)). Readers work in relays with stints of no more than two hours at a time with one always ready to take over should the person reading be taken ill. There is no difficulty in finding readers unless a *sangat* is small and has few members who can read the Guru Granth Sahib with the correct intonation.

After a ceremony called bhog, which brings the akhandpath to its close, the celebration will continue with lectures, sermons, sometimes the reading of specially composed poems, on the subject of the Guru who is being celebrated. Occasionally, the joy is shared with the local community by members of the sangat giving passers by an orange or some other fruit.

Major gurpurbs and melas according to the Nanakshahi calendar

This solar calendar will remove anomalies caused by attaching religious observances to a lunar calendar while using the Gregorian solar calendar for all other purposes. This explains why the birthday of Guru Gobind Singh can sometimes take place twice in a Gregorian year and occasionally not at all!

The major gurpurbs and melas will be as follows:

January 5	birth of Guru Gobind Singh.
April 14	Vaisakhi birth of Guru Nanak
May 2	birth of Guru Arjan
June 16	martyrdom of Guru Arjan
September 1	installation of the Guru Granth Sahib

November 24   martyrdom of Guru Tegh Bahadur

The melas of Hola Mohalla and Divali will continue to be dated according to the Bikrami Calendar.

The birthday of Guru Nanak is still likely to be celebrated in the month of Kattak/Kartik, for some years to come. (See note below.)

figure 12 at the end of an akhand path the copy of the Guru Granth Sahib which had been used may be laid to rest and replaced by another one

Hola Mohalla

Hola Mohalla has replaced Magha as the third Sikh mela.

In 1680, Guru Gobind Singh summoned his Sikhs to come to Anandpur, where he was based, not at Magha, but at the time of the Hindu Holi festival. They assembled for manoeuvres. Hola Mohalla means literally the place to attack. No translation of the

---

* The year of Guru Nanak's birth, 1469, is not in dispute but a controversy surrounds the actual birth date. Some janam sakhis give a date which would correspond to 15 April, while another tradition gives his birth not in Vaisakhi but in Kattak/Kartik, six months later. Scholars favour the spring date but observance of his birthday in November is so well established that their arguments have not affected it.

term seems particularly clear. They engaged in sieges, weapon training, mock battles and military exercises, all fitting alternatives to the frivolities of Krishna festival. Today, martial arts competitions and sporting activities are held at Anandpur. Hola Mohalla is not widely observed elsewhere, though sometimes regional hockey, football or kabbadi competitions may take place at this time.

Vaisakhi

Vaisakhi usually falls on 15 April. In Amritsar, at Vaisakhi there is a great sale of animals and many Sikhs travel on trailers behind tractors, or by bus, train and many other forms of transport to take part. This is one of the times of harvest in Punjab and it is a generally accepted Sikh tradition to celebrate Vaisakhi and then begin gathering in the grain crops. Naturally, before they set out for home they not only worship at the Harimandir Sahib but also visit other historic sites, such as Jallianwala Bagh where the massacre of 1919 intensified demands for Indian independence from the British. Remembrance of this event takes the form of political rallies and it may be wise for foreigners to visit the memorial garden in the morning rather than the afternoon when crowds may become excited, though possibly the Sikh who gave me this advice, which I heeded, was being overcautious.

The first amrit initiation ceremony was held at Anandpur; because of it the town is usually respectfully called Anandpur Sahib today. Also although the ceremony may be held anywhere and at any time, there is often an eagerness to take amrit at Anandpur on Vaisakhi, especially on the part of converts to the Sikh faith.

Throughout the Sikh world the covering (*chola*) on the flag mast (nishan sahib) outside the gurdwara will be changed at Vaisakhi. The mast will be stripped of the old, dirty chola, washed and then a new chola will be wrapped round it.

In many places where there is a large population of Sikhs, the Guru Granth Sahib will be taken around the town on a lorry or some similar open vehicle. Five men on horseback or on foot – the panj piare – carrying small nishan sahibs, will lead the procession. Children dressed as panj piare may follow and then, after the float, will come many members of the Sikh population, some walking some on carts singing kirtan to the accompaniment of musicians. This celebration is known as *nagar kirtan*. It is gradually becoming a popular public way of celebrating Vaisakhi among Sikh communities in the dispersion. There are annual reports in the press of processions where they had not been held in earlier years. They indicate communities that are becoming more self-confident in the lands in which they have settled.

At a more mundane level, Vaisakhi is usually the time when voting takes place in those gurdwaras which have elected committees.

Divali

Divali is a movable festival because it is based on the lunar calendar. This was the second *mela* to which Guru Amar Das summoned his Sikhs. It marks the end of the financial year for businessmen and women. For many north Indian Hindus, however, it principally commemorates Prince Rama's return to his capital city of Ayodhya, with his faithful wife Sita, after their years of exile. Tradition says that the inhabitants illuminated the city with lamps. These, bonfires, and fireworks, are major features of the celebrations today. Their brightness shines out all the more strongly in Indian villages because the four day festival begins at the end of the dark part of the month of Ashvina, three days before the new moon and the first day of the month of Kartik. By the Gregorian calendar this is late October or early November, though because of the complications of the Hindu leap year system there were two Divalis celebrated in one year during the 1980s. Schools and Community relations Councils in Britain were most perturbed, but the Indian High Commission phlegmatically invited people to observe whichever one suited them, and to keep both if they liked – which many Hindu and Sikh children did!

Sikhs have their own Divali story. Guru Hargobind enjoyed variable relationships with the Emperor Jehangir. Sometimes they hunted together, but in 1619 he was in prison in Gwalior. His release was ordered just before the Divali festival. The Guru refused to accept his freedom unless 52 imprisoned Hindu rajas could leave with him. The emperor agreed that he could take as many with him as could hold on to his cloak while he passed through a narrow postern gate. The Guru had long tassels attached to his cloak; the rajas held on to them and everyone was freed. His safe arrival at the Harimandir Sahib in Amritsar was welcomed by Sikhs who decorated it, and the surrounding pool, with lamps. Nowadays at Divali, the precincts of the Darbar

Sahib are outlined with electric illuminations and usually they, or traditional clay lamps and candles, will also be found on the steps and in the entrances of gurdwaras.

The fourth day of Divali is a Hindu festival dedicated to Vishvakarman and observed by craftsmen. Ramgarhia Sikhs belong to this social group. They will not be seen parading their tools and taking them to temples for dedication, but the Phagwara Ramgarhia colleges in Punjab hold their annual celebrations on this day. There seems no reason, however, to suppose that Ramgarhia Sikhs observe Divali more than any others and many of them seem oblivious to any link with Vishvakarman, so far have they moved from their Hindu roots.

Sending greeting cards is a new tradition among Sikhs and personal birthday cards is something that Asians have only begun to send since coming to Britain, often because of pressure brought by children whose friends took cards to show the teacher while they had none! If the importance of a gurpurb can be measured by it being an occasion for sending cards, the Guru Nanak's and Guru Gobind Singh's birthdays are of the greatest significance.

figure 13 langar in the open air at Patiala on the occasion of Guru Nanak's birthday gurpurb

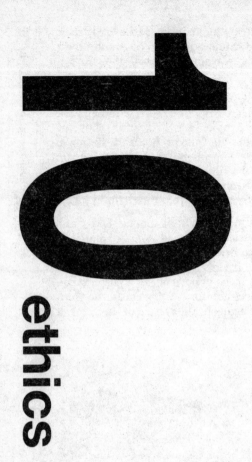

10

ethics

The way we live is related very much to the beliefs that we hold. They give us our values. Thus, a society that believes in racial superiority can discriminate against, and even enslave, members of a different race which it claims to be inferior. If women are presumed to be inferior to men, the scene is set for a system in the workplace and elsewhere that denies them promotion, and perhaps encourages sexual harassment.

Ethics, it must also be observed, are more than attitudes to particular issues, such as abortion or euthanasia. In the Indian context they relate to the whole of one's life. They are akin to the Latin *mores*, meaning 'the customs or conventions regarded as essential to, or characteristic of, a community', to quote the *Concise Oxford Dictionary*, in this respect. Westerners may distinguish between religion and culture but for many people from the Indian subcontinent, such a separation is meaningless and confusing. Although I shall concentrate on particular matters in this chapter, I must note that some of the aspects already mentioned in the section on the family are encompassed by the word 'ethics' for Sikhs, for example, to contradict one's elders or husband in public, or to look a teacher in the eye when being reprimanded. Attitudes towards arranged marriages can also be seen by Sikhs to be ethical matters.

Seva

The inseparable link between belief and conduct might best be seen in Sikh teaching about *seva*, community service. Any discussion with Sikhs about spiritual development or liberation is likely to include seva. Serving other people is a way of serving God and the Sikh who fails to respond to the presence of God in other human beings cannot possibly be *gurmukh*, God-oriented. Bhai Gurdas described a truly devout Sikh thus:

> *The hands of the gurmukh are blessed, for they toil in the service of God and the sangat. They fetch water, grind corn, and perform any service that is required of them. They copy the compositions of the Gurus and prepare hymn books, and sing to the accompaniment of musical instruments. They bow low to the Guru and embrace their fellow devotees with joy. They labour to earn an honest living, and distribute part of their income for the benefit of others. Having touched the perfect Guru, their hands have become holy, they*

will not touch the body of another woman or the
property of others. Ego and pride have been lost
through serving others. (Var 6:12)

Seva's place in spiritual liberation has been mentioned elsewhere (see Chapter 13): here its importance as the base of Sikh morality and ethics must be noted. It should not be confined to other Sikhs. However, it is learned in the family and the community 'Gurdwaras are laboratories for teaching the practice of seva' as the Rahit Maryada says, but it adds, 'the real field is the world abroad. Service recognizes no barriers of religion, caste or race. It must be offered to all'. Bhai Gurdas also said that Sikhs should be grateful to those who provide them with opportunities for seva.

Rejection of discrimination

The Sikh Gurus taught the oneness of God and the unity of humanity. In the Sikh Panth there should be no place for discrimination on any grounds, physical disability, gender, social class, skin colour or whatever else one wishes to name. As one of the Gurus said: 'We are all made of one clay'. The concept of the ritual pollution has been explained already in Chapter 02. There is no need to discuss it further but it is necessary to note that Sikh ethics is, in some respects, a reaction against the concept, though what should be stressed is the positive base of Sikh ethics stated in the first sentence of this paragraph.

Caste is perhaps the obvious issue with which to begin our study of Sikh ethics, for it was the dominant social phenomenon of Guru Nanak's day. The single word 'caste' is frequently used outside India to refer to a highly complex system of considerable social as well as religious importance. Generally it covers two words, *varna*, literally 'colour' (the fourfold divison of society into brahmins, kshatriyas, vaishyas and shudras), with the scheduled classes outside it (hence the pejorative terms outcaste or untouchable), and *jati*. It is actualy this word that is of most practical significance for the majority of Indians, including Sikhs and Christians, as well as Hindus. Jati, not to be confused with Jat, the name of the largest Sikh jati, means 'birth'. It is used as a name for the group into which one is born, status being inherited from the father. It is normally endogamous. Its place within the social hierachy of a village is determined mainly by the ritual purity or pollution derived from the group's traditional occupation. Thus, a tanner or a washerman, who are most impure because they handle animal skins and clothes which may be stained with blood or at least sweat, come low in the scale. Within a jati, (Punjabi *zat*), there are a number of exogamous kinship groups known as *gotras*, (*gots* in Punjabi). These are recognizable by their 'surname', such as Kalsi, Sambhi, or Arora. Sometimes the varna status of a group may be disputed. Not so the jati and gotra. From the early years, children are brought up to know their place and everyone else's. Guru Nanak was a *khatri*. Sometimes books say that he was a kshatriya, others describe him as a vaishya. The Sikh tendency is to place him in the kshatriya varna which is what we shall accept. The traditional family occupation was business. His jati was khatri, his gotra was Bedi. All the Gurus were khatris but only from the fourth Guru did they belong to the same gotra, Sodhi.

Even though one may change one's occupation, as many now do, for example brahmins may be surgeons or shopkeepers, as well as priests, the ritual status of purity or pollution remains unaltered. It is the consequence of birth.

The Gurus condemned the varni-jati system in strong terms. They used their influence and power to eradicate caste within the Panth. They introduced the sharing of karah parshad in which the food is distributed to everyone from the same dish, and langar, the meal at which everyone sits in the same food line, regardless of caste, though usually men and women sit in separate rows, in keeping with Indian custom.

The Gurus' attempts met with only limited success. There are a number of reasons for the survival of caste in Sikhism. One is the extended family. Today, 500 years since Guru Nanak began to preach, it is still common to find families with both Sikh and Hindu members. Family loyalty is one of the basic principles of Indian society. To marry a member of another zat would be potentially to bring the whole family into disrepute. If the person who was brought into the family in this way came from a higher zat, she or he might be acceptable to the immediate family who had arranged the marriage, but more distant relatives might find the consequences embarrassing. They might find their own children's marriages difficult to arrange. The Sikh principle has to give way to family expediency. Even if the whole family is Sikh they would still have to find a family of another zat which shares their views and is willing and able to accept a cross-zat marriage. Finally, until fairly recently, the legal code of India upheld Hindu social customs and mixed marriages across zat were illegal. Sikhs are regarded as Hindus under such legislation. Nowadays marriages across the lines of varna and zat are permissible but traditions that are probably 2000 years old are not quickly rejected. (Caste discrimination in India is now illegal but it still exists, as does illegal discrimination of various kinds in Britain and elsewhere.)

The Sikh Gurus all married within the khatri zat to which they belonged, even though Guru Arjan wished to marry his son, Hargobind, to the daughter of Chandu, a brahmin, who was finance minister to the Emperor Akbar. Chandu spoke in derogatory terms about the Guru, and Delhi Sikhs passed on his remarks to Sikhs at Guru Arjan's court. They opposed the marriage and the Guru accepted their objections. Chandu had spoken of the Guru as his social inferior and a man who mixed with low caste people to the point of eating with them. This may be only one incident but it does show that a Guru might try to disregard social convention, though not perhaps to assert the principle of equality in this case. Sikh opposition to varna and zat is based upon their belief that there is one God and one humanity. God the creator of all is accessible to everyone, regardless of caste, race, religion, or gender. In God's sight all are equal.

> *Let no one be proud of their birth. Know that we are all born from the same clay.*

The religious privileges of the brahmins came in for particular criticism from the Gurus. The Hindu tradition said that only brahmins could teach the Vedas. The Gurus rejected the idea that such a right belonged to any single group. They also denied the authority of the Vedas. They might be revealed by God but so were the utterances of such men as Kabir, Ravidas and the Muslim Sufi, Sheikh Farid, as well as, pre-eminently, the bani revealed to the Gurus themselves.

It is not easy to say how important concepts of ritual purity and pollution are in the Panth today, but one does hear of Sikhs who will bathe and change their clothes if they have visited a *chamar* (leather worker) or *chuhra* (sweeper) home. The existence of Ravidasi (chamar), and Valmiki (chuhra) congregations in Britain whose members will speak of discrimination suffered at the hands of Sikhs, may indicate a continuing concern about pollution among some Sikhs, even if the major reason is social – they look down on them as coming from a lower zat (see Chapter 16).

Sikhs are conscious that some of them fall short of the ideals of the Gurus. Reformers draw attention to their teachings and institutions, such as langar and open membership of the Khalsa, as well as the sharing of karah parshad, endorse it practically, but age-long customs are changed only slowly. A growing number of young Sikhs in Britain criticize the persistence of caste within the Panth but most of them have to bow to family pressures when it comes to marrying, and that means marrying a member of one's own zat.

Woman: male–female equality

God is without form or features according to Sikh teaching. That means it is theologically inappropriate to use he or she, him or her of God, though the terms used of God are all masculine. However bani, the word used to describe the Gurus' hymns, is a feminine noun. It is also true that Guru Nanak described himself as the bride of God saying:

> My beloved is not distant. When my soul was reconciled to the Guru I found God, the prop of my life. In this way the bride met God, the bridegroom, and became his beloved.

The name of God in this verse is Haré, one of the names of Lord Krishna, but Guru Nanak frequently used Hindu or Muslim names of God when it suited him. It did not mean that he was a Hindu or Muslim, or that he thought of God as male. On the contrary, the passage to which most weight must be given is this:

> The wise and beauteous Being (Purukh i.e. God) is neither man nor woman nor bird;

when Guru Nanak said that he was God's bride or:

> You are our mother and father, kinsman and brother;

or

> You are our mother and father, we are your children.

he was referring to a spiritual relationship of love, not one of a biological or physical kind. Such language is the common currency of mystics throughout the religions.

Gender, like all else, comes from God. It is part of creation. The Guru once said that for aeons upon aeons there was nothing but undivided darkness over which God's will held sway. At the divine command creation began. Until then there was no male or female, no varna or jati, no pain or pleasure. He also affirmed that God is hidden in and enlightens every human heart, not only those of men or only those of women.

With this as background it is not surprising that Guru Nanak stressed the importance of woman. In an Indian society that saw her as a source of spiritual pollution, where priests taught that she could not obtain liberation without being born as a man, Guru Nanak said:

> *Man is born of woman and woman of man. (AG 879)*

and

> *It is from woman that we are conceived and born. Woman is our lifelong friend who keeps the race going. Why should we despise the one who gives birth to great men? (AG 473)*

A seventeenth-century theologian, Bhai Gurdas, expressed the Sikh position as well as anyone when he said:

> *From a temporal as well as spiritual point of view woman is man's other half and assists him to salvation.*

This may seem sexist to twenty-first century readers. They must remember that he was writing to men who probably traditionally held women in low esteem and believed that they were, if anything, a threat or hindrance to liberation.

Guru Amar Das appointed women to be preachers and missionaries, realizing, no doubt, that in Muslim influenced areas of Punjab especially, women would not be allowed to speak to men who were not members of their family. But beyond the practical expediency lay the principle that women *could* preach the Sikh message. Mata Sahib Kaur provided the patashas, sugar crystals, for the first amrit initiation ceremony on Vaisakhi in 1699. This would have rendered the amrit ceremony totally unacceptable to pollution conscious men and women. She was also initiated into the newly formed Khalsa which should not be called a 'brotherhood' as it is open to women as well as men.

There were no women Gurus, it is true, but we must remember the conventions of the day which must have constrained the Gurus, and note also that the Gurus' wives often played significant roles in the development of the Panth. Principally, however, the Gurus were not social reformers but spiritual teachers and messengers. The natural corollary of what they taught may well have been the social as well as spiritual equality of man and woman but their primary aim was to preach their message of spiritual enlightenment to everyone. They could not render it unacceptable by preaching a social revolution that they could not effect.

Spiritual equality has never been denied to the Sikh woman. In religious matters the Rahit Maryada agrees that there are no functions that she may not undertake, including being one of the panj piare at the amrit ceremony. However, social attitudes often lag some way behind the teachings of the great religious preceptors and this is certainly true of the status of Sikh women. The Gurus denounced sati, the immolation of women upon their husbands' funeral pyres, and seem to have been successful in preventing the practice. Perhaps this was not too difficult because sati was such an obvious act. However, they also condemned the dowry system and female infanticide. Neither of these has been completely eradicated to this day and amniocentesis is becoming increasingly popular in Punjab, frequently leading to female foetuses being aborted. Families may also be more concerned about the sexual conduct of daughters than that of sons and more prepared to make sacrifices for a son's education than for a daughter's, attitudes not unknown in many other societies.

In Punjabi culture a girl is paraya dhan – the property of others is the literal meaning of the phrase. Her father, then her husband, are responsible for her. She is never her own person. She is a costly expense to her parents, as a dowry is expected, and after they have spent everything on her the benefit is enjoyed by the family she marries into. The rest of her life will be spent with them! Among Sikhs in the dispersion, as well as those in India who themselves have experienced higher education, a broader view of the purpose of nurturing offspring is developing, but until pension schemes replace the dependence of parents upon their sons for security in old age, change is likely to be slow and limited.

Sikh theology offers the same rights and responsibilities to women and to men. It is the powerful influence of a patriarchal society that Sikh women have to overcome. Gradually in Britain, and more so in the USA, social liberation is taking place, and in India too. There it is more common than it was to find women taking courses at university and continuing to work after marriage, but in the rural areas the old traditions may be little changed and in any Sikh community the birth of a daughter is seldom greeted with the joy that a boy baby brings, but that seems to be a response found among some members of most cultures.

Sikhs and the use of military force

The history of Sikh persecution begins with the martyrdom of Guru Arjan in 1606 and has had a strong influence on Sikh attitudes to the use of outward force. The British made use of this martial tradition by recruiting large numbers of Sikhs into the army once Punjab had been annexed in 1849. Sikhs had probably been armed since the days of Guru Hargobind (1606–44), who kept a standing army. However, it was Guru Gobind Singh, the tenth Guru, who formalized the creation of a Sikh fighting force in 1699 when he established the Khalsa, a community of Sikhs prepared to serve the Guru even to the extent of giving him their lives. This appeal for loyalty resulted in the five beloved ones, the panj piare, coming forward to offer themselves to him. The Guru asked for commitment but this was not to be of a blind unquestioning kind. He called them to observe certain principles as he did himself. He propounded the theory of the just war, the *dharam yudh*, one to be fought only in the defence of justice. Sikhs believe that Guru Gobind Singh was only following the tradition of other Gurus. The emphasis should not be upon his sanctioning the use of outward force but upon the moral pressure that he and some of his predecessors had brought to bear upon rulers. He laid down the first principle of a just war in addressing the Mughal emperor of his day. War should be a last resort. Only when all other means had failed was it right to resort to force. He communicated this rule to the Mughal Emperor, Aurangzeb, in a letter called the Zafarnama in which he accused him of tyranny. He wrote:

> When all other methods have failed it is permissible to draw the sword.

This should guide the individual Sikh who wears the kirpan (sword) as one of the five Ks. It should not be unsheathed even to show a friend what it looks like. If it is drawn, it should only be when bloodshed is unavoidable, but it should be remembered that Sikhs should be law-abiding citizens who should not take the law into their own hands.

Guru Nanak had accused Emperor Babur of injustice when he pillaged the town of Saidpur after capturing it. Guru Amar Das persuaded Emperor Akbar to end a tax on Hindu pilgrims to Hardwar. He also asked him, successfully, to remit taxes in the Labore district where his army had been campaigning and which consequently was faced with famine after crop destruction. He told members of the kshatriya class that they should fulfil their traditional obligation (sva dharma) to provide people with a protective fence of justice. Guru Hargobind had been imprisoned in a fort at Gwalior; when the Emperor Jehangir offered him his freedom he refused to accept it unless 52 Hindu rajas received similar treatment.

Justice, a basic Sikh tenet, must govern the use of force as a last resort. The other rules that relate to the conduct of a just war are:

- War should be waged without hatred for the enemy or any desire for revenge. Lust, anger, greed, attachment, and pride, are the five vices or evils that Sikhs should shun. The first four could easily be committed during a war. In a just war Sikhs should avoid them, as at all other times.
- Territory should not be annexed. Any land or property captured in the course of the war should be returned to its owner as soon as possible after hostilities have ended. Looting and the taking of booty are forbidden. This would return the motive of justice into ones of lust and greed.
- The army must be made up of soldiers committed to the cause. Mercenaries fight for greed and a share of the spoils of victory. There should be no such trophies in a just war. Rape often follows victory. Sikhs should not violate the women of their defeated enemies. Sikhs were also told that they must be disciplined in their personal lives. Members of the army should not drink or smoke or take any other drugs.
- The final just war principle is that only the minimum force necessary should be used. Once the objectives of the war have been achieved, fighting should cease and attempts should be made to establish peace.

Guru Gobind Singh, in laying down these rules, taught his followers that they should be *sant sipahi*, saint soldiers. Daily nam simran, meditation, was as much an obligation upon them as keeping their military weapons prepared. There should be a balance here as in all aspects of Sikhism where moderation is a key concept. Guru Gobind Singh once said:

*Without power, righteousness (dharam) does not
flourish, without dharam everything is crushed and
ruined.*

Protection, however, should characterize Sikh power wherever it
exists. The Sikh prayer (Ardas) ends with the sentence:

*The Khalsa shall rule, no hostile powers shall exist.
Those who come to the Khalsa for shelter will be
protected.*

The strength of the military tradition and culture in Sikhism, and
the presence of the just war theory, may be reasons for pacifism
being little discussed by Sikhs. If there are pacifist Sikhs they may
hold to their principles by not being initiated into the Khalsa.
Otherwise, in an India where there has never been conscription,
they have never needed publicly to declare themselves.

Medical issues

From earliest times Sikhs have cared for the sick by building
dispensaries and hospitals. Guru Nanak is described as healing
lepers in some janam sakhi accounts. Leprosy was a dreaded
disease at that time, and still is. It was considered incurable and
likely to be transmitted to anyone who touched a leper. Guru
Arjan set up a hospital for the care of lepers at the Punjab town
of Taran Taran. At the time, little care was available for the sick
outside the family and they were left to form support groups of
their own if they were lucky and live together until they died. The
child Guru, Har Krishan, contracted smallpox from the patients
he assisted, and died.

Medical work is still at the heart of Sikhism. Many Sikh men and
women are doctors or surgeons, still more are nurses. India is a
country that cannot afford to employ all the doctors it trains,
which explains why some of them have migrated to Europe or
America. It depends on volunteers and voluntary contributions
to make up for services that the government cannot afford to
provide. Sikhs do this by setting up clinics or dispensaries and
day wards at gurdwaras. Here, medical care is given free of
charge and minor operations can be performed.

Advances in medical research are making Sikhs think about
some other issues related to the body.

Transplant surgery

One of the great scourges of India is blindness caused by diseases of the cornea. This can be cured by corneal grafting. Sikhs are encouraged at death to donate their eyes to eye banks so that this can be done. 'Eye Camps' are set up in rural districts where patients who are blind or have poor sight can be taken and the simple operation that gives them back their sight can be carried out. In 1987, a Sikh set up a 'Life After Death' society in Calcutta 'with the object of educating the public on the necessity of donating the entire body for transplant, medical research and educational purposes, instead of cremation or burial'. (About 40,000 Indians die of kidney failure alone each year.) Mr H Singh, its convenor, wrote in the *Spokesman Weekly,* New Delhi, 20 June 1988: 'Our modest effort in the past year has led to the formation of branches in six cities including Calcutta, Bombay, and Delhi.' Transplant surgery poses no ethical problems for Sikhs.

The third Guru wrote:

> *The dead may be cremated or buried, or thrown to the*
> *dogs, or cast into the waters or down an empty well.*
> *No one knows where the soul merges and goes.*
> *(Guru, Amar Das, AG 648)*

Once someone has died the body is merely like the discarded skin of a lizard or some other animal that leaves it behind when it is outgrown. The soul or spirit has no more use for it, so it can be used for transplants or research. In practice, of course, many Sikhs would not like to think of the body of their loved ones being treated in this way, so they are only slowly accepting the idea of donating parts of the body.

Let the maximum number of Sikhs donate their eyes and other usable parts of their bodies after death by legally signing such donation papers in collaboration with local or neighbouring hospitals. In the name of the Guru, let the Sikhs sacrifice a portion of their bodies after death which he did while living. (Two Gurus were martyrs. Guru Arjan and Guru Tegh Bahadur sacrificed their lives for their faith.)

The Guru Ram Das Mission is a United Kingdom organisation which enables hospitals and eye clinics to be set up in rural Punjab. (From *Sikh Phulwari* Vol 6, no 1, July–September 1988.)

Amniocentesis

Amniocentesis is a modern clinical test that *can* be used for determining the sex of a child while it is in the womb. It is creating a problem in India where parents sometimes ask for an abortion if the child is a girl, because Indian cultures tend to prefer boys to girls. Sikhs reject this trend but some individuals may be tempted to use the test and then arrange an abortion if the foetus is shown to be female. This would be classed as infanticide, a practice which, as has already been stated, the Gurus condemned.

The Punjab census for 2001 states that the ratio of women to men in the population is now 874 per thousand. In 1991 it was 882. The most widely given reason for this is the abortion of female fetuses. The practice, as in the UK, is unlikely to be confined to Sikhs but certainly includes them.

Genetic engineering

This means the alteration of the structure of human cells. It can be a means of preventing parents passing on hereditary illnesses to their children. Many Sikhs would still feel that this was a way of tampering with the natural body which God has given. However, some doctors might argue that this was God-given knowledge that should be used to help those who suffer from these disorders. Certainly, they would approve of parents using contraceptives if they did not want to run the risk of bringing such children into the world. Once born, such a baby should be cared for with as much love as any other. He or she is a gift from God.

Sikhs would not agree to experiments being carried out on aborted foetuses as human life is believed to begin at conception.

Artificial insemination

The insemination of a wife with the sperm of someone other than her husband is morally wrong according to Sikh teachings. There is a stigma attached to it, which is akin to adultery. Even if the husband were to give consent originally and the donor were to remain anonymous, the possibility of the husband feeling inadequate and jealous would be such that the marriage could be put at risk. Adoption is the acceptable solution, or being willing to live with the childless state, acknowledging it to be God's will. For the same kinds of reasons, surrogacy is not acceptable.

In vitro fertilization, or 'test tube babies', would not be objected to by Sikhs. They would, however, look for adequate safeguards to make sure that only the sperms and ovum of a married couple are used.

Most medical ethical problems are the consequence of recent developments in the West. When to switch off a life support machine may be an issue in Delhi, Bombay and some other large cities, but often the technology to prolong life artificially is not available. This renders many issues theoretical and academic. Sikh doctors working in the West, however, are likely to be confronted increasingly by issues on which the Guru Granth Sahib provides no direct guidance. There is no evidence that their associations are as yet addressing these matters.

The rather categorical statements expressed in this section are likely to represent the views of many Sikhs in the future but doubtless some individuals and families will form their own opinions in Western societies.

the Sikh scriptures

In this chapter you will learn:

- the composition of the scriptures
- their importance
- the use of the Guru Granth Sahib in worship.

There can be no people for whom their sacred writings play a more important part in their worship and beliefs than for Sikhs. At the level of individual practice, from the naming of a child until the ceremonies in which the bereaved are comforted, the scriptures are physically present to witness and authenticate them. At the community level, no Sikh activity can take place other than in the presence of the scriptures.

The Guru Granth Sahib

The Sikh scripture is the Guru Granth Sahib. This is a compilation of spiritual poetic material composed by six of the Gurus, as well as a large body of similar material uttered by non-Sikhs, Hindus, Muslims, and some who perhaps refused to be allocated to either community. There are also some verses that were first sung by bards at the court of Guru Arjan. It contains very little historical, and only a small amount of biographical, material.

The story of the Guru Granth Sahib is one of a development which took place over a period of just over 200 years. It began with Guru Nanak who conveyed his message to villagers and others to whom he preached by means of poetry. He was not the first person in India to employ this method, or the last in the history of religions. He was one of those who recognized the value of assisting the memory by putting teaching into hymns, for which his Muslim friend, Mardana, provided easily sung tunes. Guru Nanak composed 947 hymns, which are included in the Guru Granth Sahib. The Janam Sakhis contain several others, which for one reason or another have not found their way into the scriptural collection. An example is a verse associated with his visit to Makkah in the B40 Janam Sakhi account (p. 53). They also indicate that many hymns were composed in response to particular situations. For example, the B40 also describes an incident in which the headman and qazi, a religious official, of Guru Nanak's village questioned him about his teachings. He ends the conversation by uttering the words already quoted (p. 25) in which the characteristics of a true Muslim are outlined (B40 p. 24). Other notable hymns that may be responses to particular occasions are *Siddha Gosht*, a discourse with a group of yogis, and *Arti*, which resulted from a visit to the temple of Jagganath at Puri.

At some time the decision was taken to write down the hymns of Guru Nanak. Sikh tradition is an uncertain guide in determining who was responsible. Lehna, a disciple who later became the second Guru and is better known as Guru Angad, is often credited with the achievement. It is said that he compiled the 35-letter Gurmukhi alphabet in which the scripture, and Punjabi, generally are written. Against this is the fact that Guru Nanak composed a hymn, in the form of an acrostic, making use of the 35-letter alphabet. The truth is probably that Guru Angad gave the alphabet its final form based on refinements already undertaken by his predecessor.

Of more significance than authorship is the fact that it was invented to write down the hymns of Guru Nanak. The script is called *Gurmukhi*. The word 'gurmukhi' literally means 'from the mouth of the Guru'.

Bhai Gurdas, who might be described as the first Sikh historian, writing in the days of the fifth or sixth Guru, described Guru Nanak's visit to Makkah. He said that 'he carried a staff in his hand, a book under his arm, a water pot, and a carpet for the call to prayer' (first Var, v. 32). It is likely that the book contained at least some of his hymns.

The sheer bulk of Guru Nanak's output might be sufficient reason for the decision to commit his hymns to writing, but there might be a second reason. When Guru Nanak appointed Lehna to be his successor, he passed over his two sons, Shri Chand and Lakshmi Das. Shri Chand was set up as a rival to Guru Angad, and later still to Guru Amar Das, by Sikhs who felt he should have succeeded to his father's *gaddi*. A method of winning support was to create spurious verses which would advance his claims. The natural way to counter this would be to gather the authentic hymns into a collection that had the approval of Sikhs of long and respected standing in the community.

Although the Sikh community was focused upon Guru Nanak's village of Kartarpur during his final years, there is evidence that Sikhs were to be found in other parts of Punjab. Guru Angad, himself, came from Khadur, a town some 50 miles from Kartarpur. The Janam Sakhis mention the establishment of gurdwaras (then called *dharamsalas*) even beyond the borders of India. These young communities would need copies of the Guru's hymns to use when he was not personally present with them.

We may see Guru Angad as the person who safeguarded his master's collection as a key way of consolidating the Panth. He added only 62 of his own hymns.

The compilation of the Adi Granth

The most important development in the story of the Sikh scriptures was Guru Arjan's decision to assemble in one volume an authoritative collection of authentic bani and install it in the newly completed Darbar Sahib in Amritsar. Guru Amar Das had made a beginning by encouraging his grandson, Sahans Ram, (sometimes called Sansar Ram), to gather the available material. His motives for doing so had been very much the same as those of Guru Angad. The threat from disgruntled sectarian groups was increasing, as can be seen from the warning contained in such passages as this by Guru Amar Das:

> All other teaching but that of the Sat Guru is false.
> False are those who utter it, false those who hear it,
> false those who recite and invent it. They utter the
> Name with their tongue but do not understand what
> they say. (AG 920)

There was an additional reason. Bhai Phaira, who had compiled the hymns of Guru Nanak for Guru Angad, and Bhai Budha, who had applied the ceremonial *tilak* mark to Guru Angad's forehead at his installation, were growing old and most of the first Sikhs had already died. Guru Amar Das, himself, was converted in the time of the second Guru, not the first. There was a danger that Sikhs who could witness to the authenticity of the bani would soon have passed away. Guru Amar Das, therefore, wisely revised the existing collection, adding his own 907 hymns.

Guru Ram Das composed 679 hymns but no one can approach the output of his son, Guru Arjan, the fifth Guru, who was responsible for 2218. His greatest claim to importance, however, does not relate to his poetic genius and skill, but to his decision to publish the Sikh sacred writings in one definitive volume. Guru Amar Das's revision had taken the form of at least a two volume collection. Probably there was a third volume, and maybe even a fourth, which no longer exist. These volumes (in Punjabi, *pothis*) were in the possession of Baba Mohan, the elder son of Guru Amar Das, and father of Sahans Ram who had compiled them. Guru Arjan borrowed these and also a pothi that was in the possession of Datu, a surviving son of Guru Angad. Besides using the available written sources he also had the help of the elderly Bhai Budha, survivor of the Kartarpur community, and the help of his kinsman, Bhai Gurdas, an able theologian and historian. These were entrusted with the task of determining which versions of particular hymns were to be regarded as authentic, under the careful supervision of the Guru himself. The resulting collection, known as the Adi Granth, survives in the possession of descendants of Guru Arjan at a town called Kartarpur on the river Beas, not to be confused with the village founded by Guru Nanak. Marginal comments and corrections in Guru Arjan's handwriting bear witness to the carefulness of his scrutiny.

The structure of the Adi Granth

There is no need to go into great detail but a few points must be made.

First, Guru Arjan imposed his own structure on the volume and this differed from previous ones. Using the page numbers of modern printed versions, we can say that the first 13, containing the hymns that Sikhs use every day in their private devotions, were not placed within the arrangement that is given to the rest of the book. Pages 14 to 1352 are divided into 31 sections, each named after the musical setting or *rag* to which they should be sung. The last 78 pages contain passages that are often so short, sometimes only two lines, that they could not satisfactorily be placed within the main body of the text.

The Adi Granth becomes the Guru Granth Sahib

The sixth, seventh and eighth Gurus were not inspired to compose hymns but the ninth Guru, Tegh Bahadur, and his son, Guru Gobind Singh were. In 1706, Guru Gobind Singh decided to add the bani of his father to the Adi Granth but not to include any of his own compositions. These 116 passages he placed in the rags where he thought they fitted most appropriately. Before he died in 1708, Guru Gobind Singh declared that there would be no further human Gurus. Sikhs wishing to come into the Guru's presence should come to, and listen to, the words of the scripture which would now be their Guru, the Guru Granth. Sahib is usually added as a mark of respect.

The bhagat bani

A distinctive feature of the Guru Granth Sahib is the fact that 938 shabads out of 5894 were composed by non-Sikhs. They include brahmins, Ramanand and Jaidev, and low caste men such as Ravidas, a cobbler, Sena, a barber, and Sadhna, a butcher. There was also the Muslim, Sheikh Farid, and at least one person, who would not wish to be included in any sectarian grouping, Kabir.

It was Guru Nanak who began to collect the compositions of the non-Sikh sants as they are often called. There is one important piece of evidence to support this assertion, and there may be others. It is a verse from Sheikh Farid that occurs in the Guru Granth Sahib which is cited elsewhere by Guru Nanak himself. Farid's verse reads:

> You could not make a raft at the time you should have made it. When the sea is full and overflowing it is hard to cross. Do not touch the saffron flower with your hand. Its colour will fade, my dear. First the bride herself is weak and in addition, her husband's command is hard to bear. As the milk does not return to her breast so the soul does not enter the same body again. Says Farid, O my friends, when the spouse calls, the soul departs crestfallen and this body becomes a heap of ashes. (AG 794)

Guru Nanak's rejoinder is:

> Make meditation and self control the raft by which you cross the flowing stream. Your path shall be as comfortable as if there were no ocean or overflowing stream. Your name alone is the unfading madder with which my cloak is dyed. My beloved, this colour is everlasting. The dear friends have departed, how shall they meet you? If they are united in virtue they will, and once united mortals never suffer separation again. The True One puts an end to coming and going. (AG 729)

It is impossible to doubt that Guru Nanak was aware of Farid's verse. The fact that they are not adjacent to one another in the Guru Granth Sahib is to be explained by the fact that Guru Arjan had his own reasons for placing passages where he did when he compiled the collection. His reason for separating the verses is unknown.

Whether or not Guru Nanak collected the whole of the bhagat bani cannot yet be decided. Much of the bhagat bani is in one of the Mohan Pothis, but not all, so it was clearly not Guru Arjan's decision to collect it.

Sometimes the suggestion is made that Guru Amar Das may have collected some of it. All that can be said with certainty is that the idea came from Guru Nanak. The reason for including the bhagat bani in a Sikh anthology may well have been to give practical affirmation to the basic Sikh belief that God's word is not confined to any particular religion or spiritual movement. It could also have had the effect of creating sympathy towards the Sikh movement, eventually perhaps leading to membership, from people who venerated the teachings of Sheikh Farid, Kabir and the other teachers. The fact that no material from brahminical Hindu scriptures or the Qur'an is included is easily explained. Either it could result in the charge that the Gurus were merely plagiarists or to the assertion that they did accept the authority of these scriptures. What they certainly were is eclectic in their view of scripture, refusing to claim that God spoke only through the revelation which was given to them. Although historical developments have led to the rule that only expositions of the Sikh scriptures may be given in gurdwaras, references to the sacred books of other religions may be made so long as it is with respect.

The Dasam Granth

Guru Gobind Singh did not include any of his many spiritual poetic compositions in the Guru Granth Sahib. These were collected by one of his companions, Bhai Mani Singh, in 1734. The title given to this anthology, which includes some writings by poets who served at the Guru's court, is *Dasam Granth*. It means 'collection of the Tenth Guru'. In modern printed versions, it is 1428 pages long. There was no attempt, of course, to emulate the length of the Adi Granth, which before printing varied considerably in length depending on the copyist's handwriting. Even when printing was introduced, versions varied in their extent until the 1430-page edition won official approval.

The Dasam Granth may be read in gurdwaras and some of its hymns are used in the initiation ceremony and on other occasions, but its authority is not equal to that of the Guru Granth Sahib for several reasons. It was the Guru Granth Sahib which Guru Gobind installed as Guru and that provides Sikhs with reason enough. However, it is also written in a number of languages to which many Sikhs have no access. Guru Gobind Singh was a scholar as well as a poet and seems to have been at home in the Persian of the Mughal court, the Sanskrit of brahminical Hinduism, Punjabi and other North India languages. The language of the Guru Granth Sahib may be difficult for young Sikhs living outside Punjab; the Dasam Granth presents problems for all but scholarly Sikhs worldwide.

The writings of Bhai Gurdas and Bhai Nandlal

Bhai Gurdas, (1551–1637), was a nephew of Guru Amar Das. He was a famous missionary in the Agra area and a compiler of the Adi Granth. After Guru Arjan's martyrdom in 1606 and when Guru Hargobind was a prisoner in Gwalior fort, he and Bhai Buddha were responsible for holding together the Panth. He was also a theologian, historian and poet. He composed a large number of *vars* or epic poems, hymns of praise to God's achievements through the Sikh Panth. These compositions may also be read in gurdwaras, along with those of Bhai Nandlal (1633–1713), a companion of the last Guru.

The importance of the Guru Granth Sahib

There are two ways of looking at the tremendous importance that the scriptures have for Sikhs. The first is to take note of the teachings which relate to it, the second is to consider its use by individual believers and the Sikh community. I shall begin by examining the ideas that relate to the Guru Granth Sahib.

Most obvious and immediate is the name that Sikhs use. 'Guru' informs us that the scripture is their teacher. Sikhism's scriptures, as you have noted, begin with the compositions of Guru Nanak, which were believed from the first, of Guru Nanak himself, to be divinely inspired. The story is told by Guru Nanak and Mardana, his rebeck-playing companion, walking along a road as part of a convoy of prisoners after the Mughal capture of the town of Saidpur. Guru Nanak told Mardana to prepare to play. 'I feel the bani descending', he said. Mardana was hesitant to let go the lead of a horse he had been told to look after. The Guru sharply reminded Mardana of his priorities. 'Let the horse go, the bani is descending'!

There is a statement in the Sikh scriptures themselves that Guru

Nanak uttered the bani only when inspired. He said:

> *I speak, O God, only when you inspire me to speak*
> *(AG 566);*

and:

> *As you inspire me, so I praise you, for I, an ignorant*
> *man, can say nothing myself. (AG 795)*

Sikh theology teaches that the Guru Granth Sahib is inspired scripture in the same way that Hindus believe the Vedas, Muslims the Qur'an and Christians the Bible to be inspired, not the human creation of pious and prayerful people. Before such a doctrine had been formulated, Guru Nanak and his followers held that view based on inner experience.

Whereas belief in the inspiration of the Vedas had resulted in them not being committed to writing for almost 3000 years, Sikh belief in the inspiration of the bani meant that Guru Nanak's hymns were soon written down as well as memorized. By the fifteenth century Hinduism, like Islam, was a religion with written scriptures. It was natural if not imperative for the Sikh movement to emulate the great traditions with which it was surrounded.

When Guru Arjan installed the newly completed Adi Granth in the Harimandir Sahib at Amritsar, he prostrated himself before it. In this most practical way the Guru reinforced the doctrine that the bani is of more significance than the human Guru. He was also beginning a tradition that Sikhs observe to this day. Each time they prostrate themselves when entering the presence of the Guru Granth Sahib they are also affirming its status as repository of God's word.

The word Adi is to be found in Hindu writings. 'Adi guru' means the original guru, usually God, for example. 'Adi' means first but in the cardinal rather than ordinal sense, when the word 'pehle' would be used. 'Adi Granth' is capable of being understood as a statement that the Sikh scripture can claim the same eternal quality as Hindus believe the Vedas to possess, and Muslims the Qur'an. However, a non-theological and more prosaic explanation is offered below.

The word 'sahib', which Sikhs use when they speak of the scripture, may become contentious in future. It was used respectfully in addressing, in particular, white men in the days of the Raj. The wife was known as the 'mem sahib', which indicated that her status derived from her husband.

'Sahib' is used to acknowledge the status of the scripture in the same way, but some women writers may dispense with it, claiming that it reinforces the strong but unwarranted male dominance in the Sikh Panth.

Three stories from Sikh history further enforce that Sikh view of the authority of the scripture. The first concerns a companion of Guru Arjan's, named Bhai Banno (1558–1645). When the Granth was completed in 1604, Guru Arjan deputed him to take it to Lahore for binding. On the way he stopped at his village and quickly made a copy. He had both bound and gave them to the Guru who installed the original one, which then became known as the Adi Granth to distinguish it from the Banno copy. During the process of copying, Bhai Banno added the rest of a verse by the bhagat Surdas (AG 1253 in printed versions), and retained a verse by the woman poet Mira Bhai, which the Guru had deleted. Sikhs were angered at Bhai Banno's effrontery in daring to alter the original text when they discovered what he had done and have ever since described it as the 'bitter' version compared with the 'sweet' original.

The second episode concerns Ram Rai, son of Guru Har Rai. The Guru sent his son to the Mughal court of Emperor Aurangzeb where mischief-makers told the emperor that the Sikh scriptures contained passages that were defamatory to Islam. Ram Rai was asked to explain the meaning of a verse which read:

> The dust of a Muslim is kneaded by a potter into clay
> and he converts it into pots and bricks which cry out
> as they burn. (AG 466)

Guru Nanak had been responding to followers who were arguing whether cremation or burial was the proper way to dispose of the dead. He had dismissed both groups and in doing so might flippantly have commented on the rebirth of a Muslim's body in a pot. (The best clay apparently came from burial grounds.) Ram Rai wriggled out of the difficult situation by saying that the copy that Aurangzeb had referred to must have contained a scribal error. The word 'Musulman' should have read 'beiman', which meant 'faithless'. Guru Har Rai, on hearing of his son's failure to stand by the text of the Adi Granth, said: 'The Guruship is like tiger's milk which can only be contained in a golden cup. Only he who is ready to devote his life thereto is worthy of it. Let not Ram Rai look on my face again'. Harsh words perhaps when one considers that Ram Rai was only 14 years old, but the episode conveys some idea of the significance which the Adi Granth had for Sikhs within some 50 years of its compilation.

The third account is from more recent times. In 1920, large groups of Punjabis were converting to Sikhism in the hope of improving their social status, just as centuries earlier many had become Muslims, and in the nineteenth century there had been mass conversions to Christianity. The attempt was to prove unsuccessful now, as in the past. Social tradition had a greater influence than egalitarian teaching. The converts wished to offer karah parshad at the Harimandir Sahib as was customary. But these men and women were of lower caste than was usual and there was also fear that the Panth might be diluted by so many new low caste and largely illiterate members. Reformers insisted on the openness of the religion; the karah parshad of the converts should be accepted. Traditionalists refused. It was eventually agreed to put the matter to the Guru Granth Sahib. A copy was opened at random after prayers had been offered and the following passage by Guru Arnar Das was read to the gathering:

> Upon the worthless God's grace is bestowed if they
> will serve the True Guru. Exalted is the service of the
> True Guru, to hold in remembrance the divine name.
> God offers grace and mystic union. We are worthless
> evil doers, yet the True Guru has drawn us into mystic
> union. (AG 638)

The congregation accepted the command of the Guru; the karah parshad offered by the converts was accepted.

Recently, the practice of taking a *gurmatta* has been revived. This is a method of taking decisions affecting the whole Panth by a properly constituted assembly in the presence of the Guru Granth Sahib. According to the Sikh Code of Discipline (Rahit Maryada, see page 150), the areas that might be covered are: 'subjects calculated to clarify and support the fundamental principles of Sikhism, such as safeguarding the position of the Gurus and the Guru Granth Sahib, purity of ritual and panthic organisation'. A Sarbat Khalsa, meeting of 'all the Khalsa', is a comparatively rare occurrence but the practice is yet another, and the most formal way of demonstrating the place of the Guru Granth Sahib as the focus of Sikh belief.

The significance of the Guru Granth Sahib as seen through Sikh practices

This brings together points made elsewhere in this book. It is intended to help the reader by placing them together. Details will not be repeated here.

- When one enters the diwan hall of any gurdwara, one is immediately struck by the focal position of the scripture enthroned on the *manji sahib* and under a chanani, never left unattended.
- Worshippers will prostrate themselves or bow low in front of the scripture and make offerings to it following the example of Guru Arjan. Physical respect also extends to not turning the back on the book when close to it, or sitting with the feet pointing towards it.
- Sikhs should not smoke. Other visitors are asked to leave cigarettes and other forms of tobacco outside the gurdwara. Of course, everyone's head is covered and no one wears shoes in the presence of the Guru Granth Sahib.
- At the end of the day it is customary for the Guru Granth Sahib to be closed ceremonially and it may be placed in a special room. This ceremony known as *sukhasan* is paralleled by another, parkash karna, in the morning, when it is returned to the diwan hall for installation. Sometimes the book is put to bed literally and occasionally a four-poster is used because it has an in-built canopy which serves as a chanani. Otherwise, a chanani will be hung from the ceiling. These ceremonies not only show the respect and devotion that Sikhs accord their holy book, they also demonstrate that it is to be regarded as the living word of God, not a dead letter.
- The Guru Granth Sahib is also the focus of all Sikh ceremonies. Children are brought to it for naming. Weddings must also be solemnized in the scripture's presence for them to be valid. At times of bereavement, a family will arrange a *sadharan path*, a complete but not continuous reading of the Guru Granth Sahib, lasting for some nine days at times when it is convenient for the family.
- Many Sikh families may possess their own copy of the scripture. If they do they will open it formally at random every morning and take a vak, this is a verse which gives them the Guru's guidance or command (hukam) for the day. In the evening they are likely to gather in its presence for a longer period to read it and listen to its message.

figure 14 an open Guru Granth Sahib. The printed editions which are now used in homes and gurdwaras are always 1430 pages long

- Amrit pahul, the initiation ceremony, must be performed in the scripture's presence; some of its hymns will be recited by the panj piare as they prepare amrit.
- Gurpurbs (anniversaries of the birth or death of a Guru) are marked by an akhand path. Unlike a sadharan path this is a continuous reading of the scripture which takes about 48 hours and is timed to end early on the morning of the gurpurb. Melas, the celebration of Divali and Vaisakhi, may not include an akhand path, but often the Guru Granth Sahib will be carried around the neighbourhood in procession. This is known as nagar kirtan.

Perhaps after reading this list one can begin to understand the feelings of the Sikh who asked to wash his hands before taking a gutka (anthology of texts) in his right hand to take an oath in a British court, and was told by the judge to get on with it and not waste time!

All the ceremonies mentioned above may be performed by any competent Sikh, male or female. The insistence on this ensures that the Guru Granth Sahib's authority is unrivalled. There is no priest to interpret it or monopolize the performance of ritual actions, as in some other religions. This is also a reason why translations are not installed in gurdwaras and Sikhs insist on the importance of the original language, for all translations are interpretations to some extent. It is the message contained in the book that matters. This is considered to be the word of God, meditated by the Gurus whose role was that of messenger. No human being and no ceremony should detract from the authority of the word.

Some words of Guru Arjan's placed near the end of the scripture, a passage called Mundavani, the Seal, state the Sikh belief about the value of its contents. It reads:

> *In the platter are placed three things, truth, contentment, and meditation. The nectar name of God, the support of all has also been put in it. Whoever eats this food, whoever relishes it, becomes spiritually liberated. (AG 1430)*

12

Sikh teachings about God

In this chapter you will learn:

- Sikh monotheism
- the nature of God
- God as Guru.

Sikhism is a monotheistic religion.

Perhaps because of the considerable variety of Indian beliefs about God, Guru Nanak provided a summary of his own. It is called the Mul Mantra. Tradition affirms that it was Guru Nanak's first poetic utterance, though the great scholar Professor Sahib Singh, noting that it contains the essence of his teaching, suggested that it might have been written at a later stage, perhaps when the Guru settled at Kartarpur. 'Mul' means essence and Sikhs describe it as the nearest formula they have to a credal statement. Like all the Guru's poetry, it is extremely terse in form and is difficult to translate. It may be paraphrased as follows:

ਜਪੁ ਜੀ ਸਾਹਿਬ

੧ ੳ ਸਤਿਨਾਮੁ ਕਰਤਾ ਪੁਰਖੁ
ਨਿਰਭਉ ਨਿਰਵੈਰੁ ਅਕਾਲ ਮੂਰਤਿ
ਅਜੂਨੀ ਸੈਭੰ ਗੁਰ ਪ੍ਰਸਾਦਿ ॥
॥ ਜਪੁ ॥
ਆਦਿ ਸਚੁ ਜੁਗਾਦਿ ਸਚੁ ॥
ਹੈ ਭੀ ਸਚੁ ਨਾਨਕ ਹੋਸੀ ਭੀ ਸਚੁ ॥੧॥
ਸੋਚੈ ਸੋਚਿ ਨ ਹੋਵਈ ਜੇ ਸੋਚੀ ਲਖ
ਵਾਰ ॥ ਚੁਪੈ ਚੁਪ ਨ ਹੋਵਈ
ਜੇ ਲਾਇ ਰਹਾ ਲਿਵ ਤਾਰ ॥ ਭੁਖਿਆ
ਭੁਖ ਨ ਉਤਰੀ ਜੇ ਬੰਨਾ ਪੁਰੀਆ ਭਾਰ॥
ਸਹਸ ਸਿਆਣਪਾ ਲਖ ਹੋਹਿ
ਤ ਇਕ ਨ ਚਲੈ ਨਾਲਿ ॥

figure 15 a printed form of the Mul Matra in written Punjabi. The script is known as gurmukhi

> *There is One supreme eternal reality; the true one; immanent in all beings; sustainer of all things; creator of all things; immanent in creation; without fear or enmity; not subject to time; beyond birth and death; self-manifesting; known by the Guru's grace.*

These words were placed at the beginning of the Adi Granth by Guru Arjan, its compiler. They lead into Guru Nanak's most important composition, the Japji. Their meaning will hopefully unfold in the course of the rest of this chapter but it might be appropriate to note here that 'by the Guru's grace' is a reference to God as self revealing, not to any human preceptor. In all Guru Nanak's utterances 'the Guru' is God, unless it is clear that he has some other human teacher like himself in mind.

God is One

Time and again the Gurus proclaimed that God is 'one without a second' – that means having no partner or agent through whom creation, the sustaining of the world, or liberation, was effected. Guru Nanak said:

> My God is one, truly, my God is one. (AG 350)

Guru Arjan was equally emphatic when he declared:

> Apart from God there is no other. The Lord is both creator and cause. (AG 626)

Such a view sometimes appears to be monistic:

> God is the fish and the fisherman, the water and the net, the float of the net and the bait within it. (Guru Nanak AG 23)

God is immanent and all-pervading

This is not too surprising when we remember that the Gurus were mystics and that the vision of such people is one which finds the presence of God in every experience and object. They also shared with many Hindus the belief that the atman, or *jot* (divine spark) or individual soul, is one with the Primal Soul, Brahman, though Sikhs tend not to use this particular term. Guru Amar Das spoke of the world as the image of God:

> This whole phenomenal world that you see is the visible image of God. Yes, in it I see the face of God. (AG 622)

Guru Nanak said:

> Seeing the marvel of God in nature, the mind is convinced. Through the Guru's Word one realises that all that exists is God. (AG 1043)

Sikhs, however, should not allow the belief that God is immanent within humanity or nature to become pantheism or to say that any created being is God. They are emphatically against the use of images (*murtis*) in worship though Sikhs may be found worshipping in Hindu temples especially in places where their numbers are small and there is no gurdwara. Many Sikhs, however, might look on this with disapproval, believing Hindu worship to be idolatrous.

God as Word

'*Shabad*' (or '*shabda/sabda*'), Word, is an equally rich term that Sikhs use. It is applied by Hindus to the sacred syllable 'Om', a combination of the sounds A, U, M, representing both the three Vedas and the *trimurti* of Brahma, Shiva, and Vishnu. In the Bhagavad Gita, a scripture which many Hindus revere as containing the essence of the Vedas, it says 'Om is Brahman' (8:3), the Supreme Being, and God, Krishna, commends its liberating capability. Of the devotee he says:

> '*Let him utter "Om", Brahman in one syllable,*
> *Keeping me in mind,*
> *Then, when his time is come to leave aside the body,*
> *He'll tread the highest way*' (8:13)

Brahman is the Ultimate or Supreme Reality. 'Om', the sacred syllable, is the form taken by Brahman in becoming manifest in the world. It becomes comprehensible as the Vedas which have sometimes been called *Sabda Brahman* or *Vak Brahman* to distinguish them from *Para Brahman*, Ultimate Reality (3).

'Sabda' is also an important term in the teaching of the nath yogis, a group who traced their origins to Gorakhnath, a fourteenth-century guru, but there is no need to expand further on the use of the term outside Sikhism other than to note its significance and widespread use in the Indian religious tradition.

When Sikhs use shabad, they are primarily referring to the hymns of the Guru Granth Sahib and, once one is aware of the rich meaning of the term in the Hindu tradition, it is easy to understand and appreciate the respect shown to the scripture physically as well as theologically. The Word is the manifest form of God. When a group of yogis asked Guru Nanak to name his Guru he replied:

> *The shabad is my Guru whose meditation I, the disciple, greatly love. (AG 943)*

God is self-revealing and could not otherwise be known

Sikhism shares with many religions the belief that the Ultimate Reality is beyond human comprehension and becomes known only as a result of God's self-volition. The extent of that knowledge which God discloses is also self-determined. It is enough, and no more than is needed, to make spiritual development and liberation possible. In Sikhism *Parmeshur* or *Parameshwar* to use the Sanskrit form, is the word which means the Ultimate Reality. Sikhs also use *Akal Purukh*, the Being who is beyond time, the Eternal reality, immanent in everything, but beyond human discerning. Sometimes, in Punjabi, the word jot, meaning light, is also used. 'God' is the convenient rendering that Sikhs have adopted to refer to all these terms.

God as sovereign

Sometimes religious believers seem to think that God can be manipulated by sacrifices, austere living, gifts of money, the building of lavish places in which worship may be offered. Sikhs should not hold such beliefs. Guru Nanak was unequivocal when he said:

> God cannot be told what to do. God's own will determines His actions. (AG 2)

We have already noted that there is no whimsy or mood in God's behaviour. God is self-consistent.

The names of God

Some of the many names which Sikhs use in referring to God have been mentioned already. Interestingly, they include Hindu names such as *Hari, Gopal*, and *Rama*, as well as *Allah* and *Khuda* from Islam. The Gurus seldom, if ever, employed them with Hindu or Muslim concepts in mind. They probably used them for convenience, as synonyms for 'God'. To use the word Allah when talking to Muslims would be sensible and sensitive. To use a Hindu name such as 'Krishna' would be to alienate the Muslim audience immediately. Other expressions that are more specifically Sikh are Akal Purukh, the Being Beyond Time or the Timeless One, Parmeshur, which is used in much the same sense, *Karta Purukh*, Creator, and Vahiguru. This is the popular name applied to God in conversation. Literally translated it means, 'Praise to the Guru' but more usually the phrase 'Wonderful Lord' is used. It became popular sometime after the days of Guru Nanak. Bhai Gurdas wrote:

> *Vahiguru is the Guru-mantra: by meditating on it, the filth of self-centredness (*haumai*) is removed (Var 13:2).*

The word that the Gurus used to describe God's essence was Nam, Name. Nam has various meanings. It is rather like the Greek term *logos*. Sometimes it is synonymous with 'God' as in the verse:

> *Nam sustains animal life; Nam supports the whole universe and all its parts. (AG 284)*

Or:

> *I thank the True Guru who has revealed the Name that was hidden to me. (AG 697)*

To be more precise, however, Nam is God as revealed:

> *Wherever God is manifest there is God's Name. Whatever is, that is the manifestation of God's Name. There is no place where the Name is not. (AG 4)*

Nam is also synonymous with Word (shabad), as in this passage composed by Guru Angad:

> *Without the Word how can one cross the ocean of fear? Without the Name the disease of duality has spread throughout the world. People have sunk in the ocean and perished. (AG 1125)*

There is, however, the possibility of distinction, the Word being the means of communication and the Name the object to which it points or leads:

> *One enshrines the Name in one's heart through the Word. (AG 1242)*

Nam, however, always implies power. Through meditation the latent power of God's grace is released.

The nature of God

Ultimately God is ineffable. Guru Nanak said:

> *The Lord is contained high up in the sky and down below in the nether regions too. How can I tell of the Lord? Make me understand this thing. Some rare people know what is the Name that is uttered in the mind, without the tongue. Without a doubt, words cease in such a state. That one alone understands on whom God's grace rests. (AG 1256)*

Sikhs describe God as *nirguna* and *saguna*, without form and with form, or without qualities and with them.

Guru Arjan said:

> *The Absolute Lord is formless (nirguna). (AG 387)*

but also

> *God is without qualities, (nirguna), but also with qualities (saguna): God's manifest power has overawed the entire world. (AG 287)*

As Parmeshur/Parmeshwara, the Being beyond time, God is nirguna, but being present in creation, so God also takes on form in a way.

God is also personal but care must be taken in using this statement with Sikhs. Again, Hindu beliefs and practices have significantly influenced their attitudes. The stories of Gods who are born and die and possess human foibles, as are found in Hindu mythology, make suggestions that God is personally suspect. However, God is loving and possesses many other attributes as well as a stern insistence upon social justice and high moral living. So Guru Nanak could say:

> *Nanak seeks God's protection, that of his friend, sweet as amrit. (Guru Nanak, AG 784)*

And:

> *Why do you doubt that the Creator will protect you? The One who gave you birth will also provide for your maintenance. The Creator of the world also takes care of it. (AG 724)*

Guru Arjan wrote:

> *Whatever God does is righteous and just. (AG 541)*

And:

> *No one need be afraid of God, God is just. (AG 90)*

In other words, the God of the Gurus is not quixotic and unpredictable. On the contrary, dependability is a quality of the divine that the Gurus stressed, aware, no doubt, of the uncertain behaviour that characterized many Hindu beliefs about God at the village level. Thus, Guru Angad could say:

*The One who creates and fashions the world keeps it in
its place. The Omnipotent and bounteous Creator gives
sustenance to all beings. Mortals do the work which has
been assigned to them from the beginning. Nanak says,
other than the One there is no one else. (AG 475)*

Guru Nanak condemned idolatry in a similar manner, and spoke
with sarcasm against those who worshipped idols. Apparently
he was unaware of Hindus for whom murtis are no more than
aids to worship. He said:

*Pandit, you install the image alongside its lesser
godlings. You wash it, worship it, offer it saffron,
sandalwood and flowers. You fall at its feet seeking to
propitiate it. But you beg men for what you wear and
eat! (AG 1240)*

The Sikh would give priority to immanence. Examples abound
in the Guru Granth Sahib. A few examples from the words of
Guru Nanak must suffice.

*The Lord pervades all created beings; God creates all
and assigns to all their tasks. (AG 434)*

God created nature and pervades it. (AG 84)

God is hidden in and enlightens every heart. (AG 597)

There is also a strong belief in the transcendence of God,
however, as is indicated by such a verse as the following:

*The one who creates all and whose love yokes all,
oversees it all, detached and alone. (AG 722)*

The concept of immanence is seldom far away:

*The one who permeates all hearts is transcendent too.
(AG 294)*

God as creator

That God is Karta Purukh, Creator, as well as Akal Purukh, the
Being who is beyond Time, the Eternal, is an affirmation of great
importance to the Sikh. Why, according to Sikh belief, God
should have wished to create the universe is not easy to discover.
The Gurus said:

*The Infinite One's might is enshrined in all but God is
detached and without limit or equal. God created*

nature and inanimate nature came from the existing void. From God's own Being came air, water, and the world, bodies and the divine spirit with them. Your light is within fire, water and living beings, and in your Absolute Self lies the power of creation. From the Absolute One emanated Brahma, Vishnu, and Shiva and all the ages . . .

All that springs from God merges with God again. By divine play nature was created; by the divine word the wonder was manifested. From God day and night came. From God came creation and destruction, pleasure and pain.

Again he said:

For countless aeons there was undivided darkness. There was neither earth nor sky, only the pervasive infinite Order of God (hukam) . . .

There was no Brahma, Vishnu, or Shiva. No one else but the one Lord. No female or male, no caste or birth, no suffering of pain or pleasure . . .

There was no devata temple, sacred cow or gayatri mantra . . .

No Muslim scholar or judge, no sheikhs, no pilgrims to Makkah . . .

When God wished the world was created. Without support God created the firmament . . .

By God's will the Lord has created the creation and watches over all. (AG 1035/6)

This passage makes the point very strongly, as one reads the catalogue, that in the beginning was unity. Duality was not the divine intention but has been the consequence of creation. There was no caste, there were no sheikhs or *hajjis* who divided the unity of spiritual reality in the Gurus' view. But with creation the potential for division came into existence.

God as Guru

Two very important features of Hinduism are the place of oral teaching and the emphasis upon spiritual experience. The Rig Veda, the earliest scripture of Hinduism may be dated earlier than 1000 BCE, but it was not written down fully until about 1400 CE. A belief that the sacredness of the word would be affected by it being put into writing may be one reason for this delay, another must be that the word should be transmitted or communicated by men who knew its meaning intuitively and experientially.

These men were mostly brahmins, the Laws of Manu would suggest that all were, as they said that only brahmins had a right to study and teach the vedas. However, this law code belongs to a period towards the end of the BCE era and there is evidence in the upanishads of non-brahmin teachers. Those who were brahmins might also have acted as priests but it is their role as spiritual teachers that concerns us in this essay. The name used for such men, and today some women, is guru.

Sikhs believe that the one God who cannot be known through human effort decided to communicate with humanity. To do this God took on the role of divine teacher. The divine message was given to people in every age, including the Sikh Gurus. The teaching they received was for the purpose of liberating women and men from the cycle of rebirth. It is contained in the Guru Granth Sahib.

This is the most fundamental and important Sikh teaching. This Being, God, becomes manifest as divine teacher and guide, the Sat Guru, the One who speaks the Word. In India the term 'guru' is interpreted as 'spiritual perceptor' to avoid equating it with other teachers who impart secular knowledge, but it should be realized that a guru combines the roles of spiritual guide and pastoral adviser. Deciding to marry, changing jobs, emigrating, all these are matters that one might take to one's guru. These are all matters that Sikhs should place in front of the Guru Granth Sahib and ask for its guidance.

The Sikh Gurus were men who were believed themselves to be inspired by the Sat Guru. Their claim to guruship was based solely upon this belief. Their primary function was to utter the divine word, the shabad, which they had been given. As Guru Nanak said:

> The true creator, is known by means of the shabad.
> (AG 688)

The act of creating is by God's will (hukam), but all else comes from the 'word'. Guru Nanak said:

None has encompassed your bounds, so how can I describe you using my single tongue? Whoever meditates on your true shabad is united with you. The Guru's (God's) word is a shining jewel which reveals the divine by its light ... One understands oneself and merges in the Truth through the Guru's (God's) instruction. (AG 1290)

That message, and therefore the very presence of God, is embodied in the Guru Granth Sahib.

13 human nature and spiritual liberation

In this chapter you will learn:

- human nature
- the nature of liberation
- the path to the goal.

For Sikhs, liberation is the replacement of ignorance by spiritual enlightenment. It is effected by God's grace.

Curiosity is a major reason for studying a culture. Religions often attract the attention of outsiders because of things that catch the eye – the imagination, headlines in newspapers or on TV. This is why many religions that have fairly recently come to the notice of the West are anxious about media coverage. Each has its own concerns. For Sikhs, it is being branded as militant fanatics who blow up aeroplanes or murder people by the thousand in Punjab. These issues will be taken up in Chapter 16, but here I want to point out that what really makes a Sikh should be religious faith and spirituality. The Sikh Gurus always preached that outward appearance, for example the wearing of the 5Ks and even the turban, had no importance unless they were accompanied by true, sincere devotion and ethical conduct.

But life must be based upon beliefs. We all have them. The 16-stone, 6' 7" rugby player or fast bowler may believe that he is immortal until, at about the age of 30, his strength begins to desert him. The executive who has hired and fired people by the dozen on the way to the top finds herself rich, lonely and with nothing to do at 65 when she, herself, is cast aside. 'Is that all there is to life?' she may be tempted to ask. The religions say that there is more. The believer accepts what they have to offer. The non-believer finds their solution uninteresting or unconvincing for one reason or another.

People must have followed Guru Nanak from a variety of motives. To the hard pressed, low caste villager, the Guru offered a hope of immediate liberation which the brahmin denied. This hope was open to women too. To his high caste critics it might seem like pie in the sky when the peasants died, for he could not change their present, depressed social circumstances, but he could answer that the brahmin could only offer another round of life on earth, perhaps with less drudgery and liberation at the end – hopefully, but not certainly! Guru Nanak, instead, promised the possibility of liberation now. This, however, was not merely something emotional. It was carefully reasoned.

The malady

Guru Nanak began by diagnosing the disease.

The universe is God's creation and operates in obedience to the divine will (hukam). There is no question for the Sikh of whether or not this is the best possible world God could have made. Of course it is.

The Gurus' concern was with humankind and its destiny, which was an intensely practical issue for them, and not metaphysical, theoretical distractions. For some reason, human beings alone do not live in obedience to God's will. Why?

He taught that humanity is characterized by several distinctive, one might say unique, features, which set it apart from the rest of creation.

- We have the power to discriminate between the good and the bad. We are aware of the possibility of making choices.
- We have the ability to choose between different forms of action. Our earnings can be used for gambling, for improving our home, or for helping the needy.
- We have the opportunity of entering into a conscious unity with God, through choice.

Thus the appeal of the Gurus is summed up in the following words of Guru Nanak:

> O my soul, you have emanated from the light of God, know your true essence. (AG 441)

Guru Amar Das said:

> Humanity is brimful of the nectar of God's Name. Through tasting it, its relish is known. Those who taste it become free from fear and find that God's elixir satisfies their needs. Whoever is made to drink it through divine grace is never again afflicted by death. (AG 1092)

'Brimful of God's Name' is a challenging and thought-provoking assertion. The truth of the matter, however, seems to be that most people are unaware of the presence of God in their lives and many would deny the existence of God at all. What is the explanation?

Human beings are ignorant of their origin and their true destiny. The Gurus relentlessly informed their hearers:

> You are blessed by being born human, it is an opportunity which has been given you to meet your God. (AG 378)

In other words, people are not animals who respond only to instinct. But the message often fell upon deaf ears.

The form that ignorance takes is that of holding a materialist view of the universe and basing one's conduct upon it, of behaving like intelligent animals, but animals none-the-less. At its worst it could mean a life of selfish luxury exploiting the environment and other people. It might, on the other hand, mean living a life of praiseworthy moral rectitude. Each would be equally fatal because they are really based upon putting oneself at the centre of life.

Haumai is the term that Sikhs use to account for the flaw in human personality. They will say that it comes from two words which mean 'I-I' or 'I-am-ness'. Selfishness may be an adequate rendering of haumai in many cases, but when we consider the altruistic materialist we realize that it is not wholly satisfactory. 'Self-reliance' is probably a better interpretation of the word's meaning. Often self-reliance is regarded as a great human virtue, but for Guru Nanak it was a condition which blinded people to their dependence upon God. It reduces them to the level of animal-like ignorance. The Guru even said:

> We degrade ourselves from the human order because of haumai. (AG 466)

Once Guru Nanak visited a village where a rich moneylender lived. Periodically he counted his wealth and when he passed another landmark on his way to becoming a millionaire he would erect another pennant to let everyone share in the knowledge of his success. The Guru gave him a needle and asked him to keep it safe until he could return it to the Guru in the next world. Only when the man's wife ridiculed him did he realize that material objects cannot be taken with us and cease to have value when we die. The man's ignorance was dispelled, he gave away his wealth to those in need and became the Guru's disciple.

The following verse probably sums up our discussion on haumai as adequately as any:

> In haumai one fails to perceive the real nature of liberation. In haumai there is worldly attachment (maya) and doubt, its shadow. By acting under the influence of haumai humans cause themselves to be born repeatedly. If haumai is understood the door of liberation can be found but otherwise there is argument and dispute. Our karma is inscribed

*according to the divine will. Whoever sees the nature
of the divine will perceive the nature of haumai too.
(AG 466)*

Human beings are *man-mukh*, self-centred.

Maya is a rich term in Indian philosophy. For Sikhs the world is
not an illusion as some Hindu philosophers teach. The created
universe that God has made for man to enjoy is real. Maya
means the temporal world and human attachment to it, hence
the translation 'worldly attachment' in the passage quoted
above.

Attachments may be of a socially acceptable kind. Yet love of
family, even service of the gurdwara, or patriotism, can be
examples of maya, wrong attachment. Devotion to family can
blind a person to the higher devotion, which is to God. 'My
country right or wrong' can lead to the sanctioning of all kinds
of atrocities. Sitting on gurdwara committees, looking after the
accounts, preparing schemes for extensions to the existing
building, can be so all-absorbing that one has no time to enter
the diwan hall and listen to the bani. It becomes background
music, relayed by the loud-speaker system.

Usually when Sikhs think of maya more obvious manifestations
come to mind, especially the five evils of *kam*, *lobh*, *moh*, *krodh*
and *ahankar*. These are lust, covetousness, attachment, wrath,
and pride. Each one might be seen as an acceptable quality which
has got out of control. Haumai turns love to lust or
covetousness, as possessiveness replaces an affection which puts
the beloved before oneself, and so it is with the other evils. As
Guru Nanak said:

> *The love of worldly values stretches over the whole
> world. Seeing a beautiful woman a man covets her.
> With his sons and gold man increases his love. He
> considers everything to be his own. He does not heed
> God. (AG 1342)*

The potential for attachment to maya is present from the
beginning of time. The possibility of being attached to the world
is the consequence of being born as a discriminating human
being able to make choices. Maya like the rest of creation, is the
consequence of God's will or hukam, but because we might fall
victim to it we cannot blame God any more than an ambulance
crew collecting a patient from a house in an emergency can be
blamed for the actions of a young person who climbs into the

empty cab, drives it away and causes an accident. Such attachment is the lot of most people. Guru Amar Das said:

> *A child is born when it pleases God and the family is happy. Love of God departs, greed attaches itself to the child and maya's writ begins to run. God is forgotten, worldly love wells up and one becomes attached to the love of another (instead of God). Those who enshrine love for God, by grace, obtain the divine being in the midst of maya. Nanak says, those who enshrine love for God in their hearts, through the Guru's grace, obtain God even in the midst of mammon. (AG 921)*

You might consider whether the word delusion might be the most satisfactory translation of maya when the Sikh Gurus use it.

The remedy: the path to spiritual liberation

Put simply, what must be done to achieve liberation is reversing the process which has led to a person being ensnared and so living under the rule of haumai. One must become gur-mukh, God centred, instead of being man-mukh, self-centred.

To some extent this can be achieved by human effort. The Janam Sakhis contain many accounts which demonstrate this. For example, there was a man called Sajjan. He gave shelter to pilgrims, even providing a mosque and mandir as places for Muslims and Hindus respectively to pray and sleep. In the middle of the night he would kill them and take what possessions they had. Sometimes these might be considerable, carefully hoarded savings that they were taking to give at the place of pilgrimage. Guru Nanak and his friend Mardana accepted his hospitality but instead of going to sleep they stayed awake singing hymns well into the night. Eventually, Sajjan began to listen to their words and became captivated by the message of liberation that they contained. At last, he burst in upon the singers and asked to become a Sikh.

This story is pregnant with meaning. It speaks about the power of the bani to transform the listener, it implies the power of God's grace, it gives some indication of the need for effort on the part of the would-be reformed person. Sajjan had to wish sincerely to be changed. It also affirms the Sikh belief that spiritual enlightenment should result in a transformed life, as the former murderer was required to pay restitution to the relatives of the people he had bereaved and, after building the first gurdwara (known in those days as a dharamsala), gave the rest of his money to the poor.

The effort that Sajjan made was to put his self-centredness behind him and re-focus his attention on Guru Nanak, and through him on God in the form of the hymns that he heard. Human striving has its place but only up to a point. Guru Nanak taught that:

> Good actions may result in a human form, but liberation comes only from God's grace (AG 2);

and,

> God cannot be won through rites or deeds. Learning cannot give help in comprehending God. The Vedas and eighteen Puranas have failed to reveal the mystery. That comes only from the True God. (AG 155)

Grace

The word 'grace' is used to translate a number of Punjabi words. One of these is *darshan*. This is used to describe or refer to the benign glance which a guru bestows on a disciple. It is more than a friendly look. It is powerful and transforming, conveying peace or energy, and enlightenment. Darshan cannot be obtained, it has to be bestowed. In other words, darshan is given by the guru only to those who are deemed ready to receive it. Simply to see a guru is not to receive darshan.

Five stages of development on the path to enlightenment

In his famous Japji, Guru Nanak described five *khands* or realms through which the personality passes on its way to oneness with God. Scholars have found it difficult to agree on their precise meaning so in other books you may come across different interpretations.

Dharam Khand

The first stage is *Dharam Khand*, the realm of duty or piety. This is Guru Nanak's description of it:

> God created the night and day, the days of the week and the seasons of the year. With them he created wind and water, fire and the regions established below. Amidst them all he set the earth, the place where men are confronted by duty. Wondrous the creatures there created, boundless variety, countless their names. Each must be judged by the deeds he performs, by a faultless judge in a perfect court. Those who are justified stand radiant in glory, bearing upon them the mark of his grace. All who enter are recognised, Nanak, the false distinguished from those who are pure. Such is the Realm of Duty.

This is the world into which all human beings are born. This is where we are challenged to live according to our understanding of duty and responsibility. Those who satisfactorily live according to the basic standards of duty receive grace and proceed further.

Gyan Khand

Gyan Khand, the realm of awareness, or knowledge is described as follows:

> Hear now the Realm of Knowledge – the infinite variety of wind, water, fire, numberless Krishnas, countless Shivas, endless Brahmas creating endless lifestyles of form, of colour, of outward attire. All are present in infinite array – the earth and sacred mountains, each with its Druva uttering sermons without end; the Indras, the moons, the suns, infinite spheres and lands without number; Siddhs and Buddhas, Naths, and devis, gods and demons, men of silence, precious jewels and mighty oceans! How deep the mines, how varied the speech, how grand the dynasties of rulers and kings! Infinite forms of meditation, numberless those who perform them. Boundless, limitless, infinite, O Nanak. None can perceive its end. Enlightenment shines in the Realm of Knowledge, music and spectacle, wonder and joy.

Mind expansion seems to characterize this stage. Having passed beyond the narrow limits of dutiful, earthbound, mundane living the devotee is mind-blown by a new vision of reality.

Karam Khand

> *Beauty prevails in the Realm of Endeavour, beauty of form, unique in its splendour. Words will not serve, for none can describe it. Were one to try one would surely be humbled. Perception is sharpened, wisdom grows deeper, powers far transcending the knowledge of mortals.*

Human skill and effort reaches its limits as the new vision of reality includes aesthetic awareness. Knowledge becomes something much more profound, wisdom.

Saram Khand

> *Mastery rules in the Realm of Grace, for there God's will prevails. There one encounters mighty heroes, filled with the spirit of God's pervading power; and the virtuous women, praised as was Sita, women of beauty no words can describe. Death cannot touch them or any deceit, for God resides in their hearts. God also dwells in the hearts of his faithful, host upon host enraptured by his presence.*

God's prevailing power is grace. It is this which creates truly beautiful people and heroes who are personified by Sita, whose virtue overcame the evil demon Ravana in Hindu mythology, and her husband's lack of trust that she had remained faithful during her imprisonment.

Sach Khand

> *God's ultimate dwelling is the Realm of Truth, the ineffable home of eternal bliss. There the Creator keeps watch over all, imparting grace, bestowing joy. Within that realm are continents and universes, their vastness far beyond power of telling. Worlds upon worlds and endless forms, all of them acting as God has decreed. Joyously God watches, guiding their courses. To describe them, Nanak, is hard as steel.*

The vision mentioned in the second stage becomes reality as the soul takes its place with God in the realm of eternal bliss. Infinity has been entered. The spirit seems to be seeing the universe no longer from a human, but a divine, perspective. This state can only be experienced, not described.

Jivan mukt

Liberation here and now. Guru Nanak didn't offer pie in the sky when you die. Once the veil of ignorance is removed and God's grace becomes active it is possible to achieve liberation in this present life. Self-centredness is replaced by God-centredness. A person becomes God-filled. We quoted earlier the words of Guru Amar Das that human beings are 'brimful of the nectar of God'. Now that the self-imposed obstacles to being aware of that startling fact have been removed the potentiality for enlightenment becomes a reality. Such a person will accumulate no more karma. The consequences of earlier actions, however, will continue to have an effect but death, when it comes, will be only like a snake sloughing off its skin. To change the metaphor, it is like the passing of the night as the soul enters a new day.

Sikhism in the modern period

In this chapter you will learn:

- modern movements
- responses to external challenges
- definitions of orthodoxy.

The death of Guru Gobind Singh heralded a century of suffering for the Sikhs. It is said that during the eighteenth century the home of Sikhs was in their saddles. The declining Mughal Empire was faced with rebellion by many of its subjects, including the Sikhs. The struggle began as soon as 1710 when one of the Guru Gobind Singh's companions, Banda Singh, raised the standard of revolt in Punjab. The Mughal response was an edict that 'disciples of Nanak' were to be killed wherever they were found.

Warfare is never clean. Mughals would point to examples of the Sikhs not keeping to the rules laid down by Guru Gobind Singh. Sikhs, on their part tell the story of the execution of Banda Singh and his followers after their capture in 1716. He was compelled to see his captured followers executed over a period of days, then he was tortured for three months because the Mughal officials believed that he had a huge treasure hidden somewhere. His commanders and his four-year-old son were killed in front of him and when he finally refused the offer of his life in exchange for converting to Islam, he, too, was put to death.

Towards the end of the century, Sikh armies gained the initiative. In 1799, the city of Lahore fell to a 19-year-old general, Ranjit Singh, who made it the capital of an empire that covered the whole of the geographical area of Punjab and, on occasions threatened to include Delhi. Maharaja Ranjit Singh ruled an independent state until his death in 1849 when the British annexed the territory. Maharaja Ranjit Singh had been a tolerant ruler. He employed Muslims in such important offices as chief minister, personal physician and police administrator of Lahore. A Hindu was palace chamberlain. Westerners advised him on the organization of his army. Some Sikhs look back to this period with pride, others, however, note that he was so easygoing in matters of religion and personal conduct (for example, he had several wives, and the Hindus among them committed sati – that is, they immolated themselves on the funeral pyre – when he was cremated). Bearing such things in mind, some historians consider his reign to have contributed more to the decline of Sikhism than to its consolidation.

In India, and occasionally in Britain, blue-uniformed and yellow-sashed men and women, and sometimes children, may be seen, heavily armed with bows and arrows, spears and kirpans. In Punjab they may carry automatic rifles. These are *nihangs*. They fought almost as suicide squads in the army of Guru Gobind

Singh, and, in the eighteenth century, operated as cavalry units against the Mughals and Afghans. Later, they were involved in the struggle to recover gurdwaras from Hindu control. They are often regarded as a relic of bygone days and their encampments in India, where they shun the comfort of houses, might best be avoided by non-Sikhs. Their continued existence, however, is a reminder of struggles in the past that Sikhs cannot forget and which no one who wishes to understand Sikhs today can afford to ignore.

Religious matters

Perhaps the distinction is somewhat Western and Sikhs might not accept it for there is usually no religious-secular division in India life; it is intended to help the non-Sikh reader.

Sikhism in the early nineteenth century seems to have lacked religious cohesion and unity. Leaders like Banda Singh and Ranjit Singh had provided a political focus but there was no one to meet the spiritual needs of the Panth. In fact, Guru Gobind Singh had left explicit instructions that his successor in this respect should be the Guru Granth Sahib and the Khalsa. There were to be no more spiritual leaders.

In times of unrest the Panth seems to have remained small. Only those who were committed to the teachings of the Gurus would call themselves Sikhs when the price of allegiance might be death. In such circumstances, gurdwaras and other Sikh property often passed into the possession of non-Sikhs, or their owners concealed themselves as Hindus who were much less oppressed than the Sikhs. Some owners were nominal Sikhs, converts of convenience who did not really adopt the Sikh beliefs and practices but hoped that under the rule of a Sikh Maharaja they might benefit from becoming Sikhs. For whatever reasons, the reign of Maharaja Ranjit Singh found gurdwaras in Hindu control, Sikh weddings being conducted by brahmins according to Hindu rites, and the Guru Granth Sahib, if it was installed at all, sharing the diwan hall with murtis of Hindu deities. Eventually, a religious revival took place.

The Nirankari movement

It was into this situation that Dayal Das, also known as Baba Dayal, grew up. He was born in 1783 in Peshawar and died in

1855. At the age of 18, when he was waving the *chauri* over the Guru Granth Sahib, he went into deep meditation and heard a voice speaking to him. It told him to cease the ritual practice in which he was engaged, and recognize and preach the message of God as *Nirankar*, the formless one. This he began to do using as his slogan:

> *All glory to the Formless One; a God corporeal you must shun.*

This message was not always popular in the Punjab of Maharaja Ranjit Singh because it was accompanied by attempts to purify Sikhism of Hindu practices. For example, Baba Dayal called Sikhs back to the use of Sikh post-funeral rites as opposed to the Hindu practices which many of them had adopted. This led to conflict with those Sikhs who saw nothing wrong in them and with Hindus who were paid a fee to perform the ceremonies. The spirit of religious harmony and tolerance which the Maharaja promoted seemed threatened. Baba Dayal believed that the Guru Granth Sahib should be the only visible focus for Sikhs. He revived the use of the Lavan wedding hymn (see pages 65ff) and refused to allow brahmins to conduct Sikh ceremonies. According to the 1891 census there were 60,000 Nirankaris in Punjab. There can be no doubt that they provided one of the reforming resistance movements to the teachings of Christians and Hindu Arya Samajists during the second half of the nineteenth century.

Baba Dayal rejected the militant Khalsa ideal which he regarded as conflicting with the spiritual teachings of Guru Nanak. For this reason Nirankaris are sometimes called Nanak Panthis, though this term might be used by other Sikhs. His followers have developed a line of Gurus. Today many Nirankaris take amrit or are keshdhari. However, they wish people to accept the teachings of the Guru Granth Sahib, which is a touchstone for living and do not want insistence on the outward form to stand in the way of this. The headquarters of the movement is in Chandigarh. On 18 Marg, (at the end of January) they remember the death of Guru Dayal Das with a night long kirtan and gurbani recital.

They should not be confused with the Sant Nirankaris Mandal based in Delhi which is not Sikh and whose teachings run contrary to Sikh dharam.

Namdharis

This is the name of a similar reform movement though, unlike the Nirankaris, they could sometimes resort to physical force to make their point. Baba Ram Singh (1816–84) was their chief protagonist, though the pioneer of the movement was Baba Balak Singh (1799–1861). Initially, their opposition was to moral laxity, the use of drugs and alcohol, and personal extravagance in the celebration of marriages, all of which the Gurus explicitly forbade. They also denounced dowries, the observance of caste in arranging marriages, and the practice of forbidding widows to remarry. In all these matters they were also upholding the known teachings of the Gurus. Their advocacy of vegetarianism, and with it a certain support for the concepts of ritual purity and pollution, however, were not precepts given by the Gurus. Namdharis became involved in the independence struggle and a number of them were executed by the British for attacking Muslim slaughter-houses and butchers' shops in the campaign to restore Sikh rule to Punjab during the 1870s. Their leader, Baba Ram Singh, was not implicated in the disturbances but, nevertheless, was exiled to Rangoon.

Namdharis have been led by a series of Gurus since the banishment of Ram Singh, the present leader is Guru Jagjit Singh Maharaj. One day Guru Ram Singh will return at the end of a period of turmoil. There will be an age of righteousness when humanity will live according to the universal principles preached by the Gurus, though not everyone will necessarily be Sikh.

Their headquarters is at Bhaini Sahib in Punjab. They celebrate the gurpurbs of their own Gurus; that of Guru Ram Singh on Vasant Panchami or Saraswati Puja, the first day of spring in February; Guru Balak Singh's which coincides with Hola Mohalla; and Guru Jagir Singh's two days before Guru Nanak's birthday.

Each of these movements strengthened the Panth and brought it back to an awareness of Sikh principles some years before another reformist group, the Singh Sabha movement came into existence in 1873.

The Singh Sabha movement

Reabsorption into Hinduism has always been, and still remains, a perceived threat to many Sikhs, and the Nirankaris and

Namdharis did much to counter it in the nineteenth century. However, another development was to cause them even greater anxiety, though eventually it led to a Sikh renaissance.

In 1834, the American Ludhiana Mission began its work in Punjab. It brought the printing press with it and published the New Testament in Punjabi. It met with little success until 1873 when four Sikh students of Amritsar Mission School declared their intention to be baptized. Such conversions as had previously occurred had been among low caste, mostly illiterate, Sikhs.

The success of Christians among educated, wealthier, and higher caste Sikhs in Amritsar, the religious centre of Sikhism, caused shock and panic. Thakur Singh Sandwalia and Giani Gian Singh decided upon a response which became known as the Singh Sabha Movement. The Amritsar Singh Sabha was formed on 1 October 1873 and others followed in the next few years. These associations (sabha means association), had a number of aims:

- to restore Sikhism to its original purity, free from Hindu influences
- to publish books on Sikh history and religion
- to establish journals and newspapers in Punjabi
- to bring apostates back into the Panth
- to interest the British in their educational programme and win their assistance in establishing Sikh educational institutions.

The Arya Samaj

No sooner had the Sikhs begun to counter the Christian threat than another Hindu challenge developed. In 1877, the Arya Samaj, a Hindu reform movement, became active in Punjab.

The Arya Samaj is a society dedicated to the restoration of pure vedic religion. It is the outcome of the insight of one man more than any others, Dayananda Saraswati, who was born in Gujarat in 1824 into a Shaivaite brahmin family. He came to reject the idea of image worship. He began to question other aspects of his tradition and set off to live the life of a sadhu. He learned yoga and found a guru, Virjananda Saraswati, who required him to vow to reform Hinduism of its impurities, image worship, avatar, (the doctrine of divine incarnation), and the ideas contained in the puranas, the myths which provide a basis for popular Hinduism. In 1875, he founded the Arya Samaj and led it until his death in 1883.

Dayananda summed up his teaching, which became Arya Samaj doctrine, as follows:

> *I hold that alone to be acceptable which is worthy of being believed by all men in all ages. I do not entertain the least idea of founding a new religion or sect. My sole aim is to believe in truth and help others to believe in it, to reject falsehood and to help others in doing the same.*

He taught that the Vedas insisted upon the treatment of all other human beings with love and justice in accordance with their merits.

The most important consequences of this teaching were the rejection of caste and eventually of discrimination against women, accompanied by programmes of social reform, the establishment of schools and colleges so that the poor and socially disadvantaged could obtain an education, and, above all, the assertion that the criterion of truth was the Vedas as they interpreted them. This brought them into conflict with the Sikhs in Punjab where, for a time a Sikh–Arya alliance against the Christian missionaries seemed a possibility. After all, many of his ideas had been taught by the Sikh Gurus centuries earlier.

Arya missionaries went around the villages persuading people to take part in a *shuddhi* purificatory thread ceremony. They were particularly successful in winning people of low caste and seemed to threaten the very existence of the Sikh religion, until the Singh Sabha movement struck back through its educational programmes.

The Sikh response was the creation of more Singh Sabhas. These were eventually coordinated in 1902 under the Chief Khalsa Diwan, a council pledged to cultivate loyalty to the British crown and to safeguard Sikh rights. During the period between 1873 and 1902, Sikh schools and colleges, often called Khalsa colleges, were established with the support of British administrators who saw the value of Sikh loyalty and the worth of harnessing the Sikh martial tradition to service in the British army. This, in turn, promoted Sikh identity as it became a rule that Sikh soldiers must be keshdhari.

Chief among sympathetic Britons might be Max Macauliffe whose six-volume history of the Sikhs during the period of the ten Gurus is still in print and widely read. He is the best known of a number of British administrators who made studies of the Sikhs.

British support also led to the passing of the Anand Marriage Act of 1909, which legalized the practice restored by Baba Dayal Das two generations earlier. Until then Sikhs were supposed to have Hindu weddings. In 1925, the Gurdwaras Act gave Sikhs control of gurdwaras in the area of historic Punjab, taking them from the Hindus who had often possessed them for more than a century. Actual administration of the gurdwaras was placed in the hands of an elected body, the Shromani Gurdwara Parbandhak Committee (SGPC), which had been established in 1920.

There was still little agreement on what Sikhism was in practice. Writers such as the scholar Bhai Kahn Singh wrote books like 'Sikhs . . .We are not Hindus' (1899) as part of the Singh Sabha movement's redefinition of Sikhism in terms of what the Gurus had taught. It was written to provide Sikhs with evidence, from the writings of the Gurus, that Sikhism had its own distinctive teachings, in the hope that they would return to what were considered to be the pure beliefs and practices of the period when the Gurus guided the Panth.

The Rahit Maryada

The Rahit Maryada is usually translated into English as The Sikh Code of Discipline or The Sikh Code of Conduct. It was approved by the SGPC in 1945 after some 14 years of deliberation and drafting. Guru Gobind Singh had provided the Khalsa with a code of discipline when he instituted it, but its precise details have been a matter of argument among members of the Panth. Since the eighteenth century a number of codes (*Rahit Namas*) have been produced, often claiming to be authorized by the tenth Guru, but they have sometimes contained material clearly at variance with the Guru's known teachings. For example, the Chaupa Singh Rahit Nama, ascribed to a brahmin Sikh of that name living in the days of the Guru, states that Sikh marriages should be performed by a brahmin and that brahmins should receive twice the deference paid to any other Sikh!

The Rahit Maryada is divided into a number of sections. It begins with instructions on personal devotion, then provides a version of the congregational prayer, Ardas; it goes on to give rules for gurdwara worship and the reading of the Guru Granth Sahib, followed by a list of beliefs and prohibited practices. The second section covers naming, marriage and death ceremonies. The subjects of the third part are seva, langar and amrit pahul.

The Rahit Maryada is a code which upholds the Khalsa ideal and has won widespread support worldwide. It is usually consulted when there is any doubt upon the correct observance of ceremonies.

As the brief outline given above shows, much of the Rahit Maryada relates to a Khalsa Sikh's individual beliefs and conduct. Most of it, however, is of value to gurdwara committees which are responsible for the orderly conduct of worship and ceremonies. It informs them how all the ceremonies for which they are responsible should be conducted and warns them against non-Sikh practices that are likely to be included if reliance is placed upon folk traditions. The main reasons for the attempt to produce it were to enable the Panth to be faithful to the perceived teachings of Guru Gobind Singh, to provide uniformity of belief and practice, and to rid it of non-Sikh teachings and rituals. The last two of these aims are of special importance for gurdwaras outside India.

A typical gurdwara in the USA or UK caters for Sikhs from many parts of the Punjab, and often from East Africa as well. They are likely to have experienced many differences in practices. They may seem minor, for example, the placing of incense sticks and a small dish of water near the Guru Granth Sahib, but they can have considerable controversial potential. One group of Sikhs will say that they are Hindu practices which Sikhs should reject. Others will say that they have been part of the custom of their village gurdwara or home throughout living memory. The Rahit Maryada can be consulted for a definitive judgement. Sometimes women are not permitted to read the Guru Granth Sahib in the sangat; other gurdwaras may discourage them during menstruation. The Rahit Maryada does not give precise instructions on this matter but its guidance is clear – women may perform any ceremonies, and the concept of ritual pollution has no place in Sikh teaching. The conclusion to be drawn is that women may act as readers of the scripture at any time.

Arguments may occur over the conduct of the amrit ceremony. It may rarely take place in some villages, if at all. The Rahit Maryada provides the committee with details of how it should be conducted, though in such circumstances they might defer to the experience of another sangat where members have performed the ceremony.

One Sikh wanted to hold a family wedding in the afternoon because relatives had long distances to travel. The community disapproved. The tradition is to hold weddings before noon, perhaps to counter Hindu-influenced ideas of auspicious times. The Rahit Maryada gave no advice, but because it did explicitly reject notions of auspicious times, the Sikh successfully argued that convenience should be the deciding factor and the wedding took place in the afternoon.

The difficulty facing the Panth is that it has no organizational hierarchy or authority to which it can turn. The five *takhts* in Punjab were established for this purpose but they are far from London, New York or Sydney and, strictly speaking, they have no authority beyond Punjab, only moral pressure. The Rahit Maryada is more conveniently available and free from the personal views that a jathedar of a takht is capable of giving.

By and large, the Rahit Maryada does provide a yardstick by which gurdwaras measure and decide their practices. Often they use Teja Singh's *Sikhism: its Ideals and Institutions* for further guidance. It was published in 1938 and its author clearly influenced the final form of the Rahit Maryada.

There are at least two matters that the Code of Discipline does not deal with. First, it does not define a Sikh precisely, though this is often remedied by appending to copies definitions from the 1925 and Delhi Gurdwaras Acts. Secondly, it does not say who may be elected to gurdwara committees or who may vote at elections. These issues are wisely left for local decision.

The power of local caste groups, families or sants, lies beyond the ability of a book to control, but the cohesion of the Panth and the general uniformity of Sikh practice worldwide owes much to the effectiveness of the Rahit Maryada.

Jathedars and takhts

The term jathedar originally referred to the leader of a group of Sikh volunteers, a *jatha*, usually soldiers who gave themselves to the full-time service of the Panth. 'Captain' might be an English equivalent. Now it is used of the head of one of the five Sikh takhts. He is a paid official chosen by the SGPC to serve for an indefinite period. He (no woman has yet been appointed) may issue hukam namas but should only do so after a panthic conference.

Takhts, literally thrones, are seats of temporal authority. Five gurdwaras are described as takhts. They are:

- Akal Takht, Amritsar, established by Guru Hargobind opposite the focus of spiritual authority, the Adi Granth, housed in the Harmandir Sahib.
- Patna Sahib in Bihar, where Guru Gobind Singh was born.
- Keshgarh at Anandpur, where the first amrit ceremony was held.
- Nander, near Hyderabad, where Guru Gobind Singh died.
- Damdama Sahib, near Bathinde. This was only declared to be a takht in 1966. Guru Gobind Singh spent some time there during which he completed the final recension of the Guru Granth Sahib.

The purpose of jathedars and takhts is not clearly defined. The jathedars sometimes assumed political roles and occasionally made doctrinal statements which should be pronounced by the whole Panth gathered in the presence of the Guru Granth Sahib. Such a gathering, known as a *sarbat khalsa* is not practicable, especially when 16 million Sikhs live in so many countries. Where authority lies in Sikhism is a difficult question to answer as anyone who has tried to involve Sikhs in meetings of religious leaders knows. In practice, it is in the Guru Granth Sahib and the accepted guidance of the Rahit Maryada. At local level, it lies in the sangat or those chosen to lead it or speak for it.

Sometimes the media describes jathedars as Sikh high priests and the Akal Takht has been called the Sikh Vatican. It should be clear by now that the idea of a clergy and priesthood and anything approaching a papacy makes a nonsense of everything the Gurus taught and their followers believe.

Should an international Sikh governmental organization exist? It will be for Sikhs to decide how this question should be answered, not because outsiders would like a body with which councils of Christian churches can confer, but because Sikhs themselves feel the need for one. They are unlikely to be pressurized by developments in other religions to conform and break with their own principles.

Defining orthodoxy

The parameters of orthodoxy are matters of perennial concern within religions, though they may go unnoticed by the outside world. Contemporary societies are generally more liberal and tolerant than those of the past when heretics, those who held views unacceptable to established canons of orthodoxy, were imprisoned or even put to death. Some people might argue that this results from the weakening of religious power rather than enlightenment, of course. However, the fundamental issue of defining such words as 'Jew', 'Muslim', 'Sikh' or 'Christian' remains.

The definition of 'Sikh' was formalized in the Sikh Gurdwaras Act of 1925.

> *Sikh means a person who professes the Sikh religion or, in the case of a deceased person, who professed the Sikh religion or was known to be a Sikh during his lifetime. If any question arises as to whether any living person is a Sikh, he shall be deemed respectively to be or not be a Sikh according as he makes or refuses to make in such a manner as the State Government may prescribe the following declaration:*
> *'I solemnly affirm that I am a Sikh, that I believe in the Guru Granth Sahib, that I believe in the Ten Gurus, and that I have no other religion'.*

The Gurdwaras Act gave custody of the historic gurdwaras of the Punjab to the Panth through the elected SGPC. Some kind of definition was necessary to decide who had the right to vote or stand in elections to the SGPC. The concern about 'a deceased person' had to do with property rights. It was caused by the ownership of many gurdwaras being in the hands of Hindu families as ancestral possessions. A conversion of convenience could result in such families retaining ownership and thus being able to perpetuate the kinds of practices found in Hindu temples. The Act tried to provide safeguards to meet this possibility. The 1971 Delhi Gurdwaras Act, giving control of its gurdwaras to an elected Delhi SGPC, added greater precision to the 1925 definition. It reads:

> *Sikh means a person who professes the Sikh religion, believes and follows the teachings of Sri Guru Granth Sahib and the Ten Gurus only, and keeps unshorn hair. For the purposes of this Act, if anyone poses the*

question whether a living person is a Sikh or not, he
shall be deemed respectively to be a Sikh according as
he makes or refuses to make in the manner prescribed
by rules the following declaration:
'I solemnly affirm that I am a Keshdhari Sikh, that I
believe in and follow the teachings of Sri Guru Granth
Sahib and the Ten Gurus only, and that I have no
other religion'.

Three aspects of these statements might be noted. First, the
movement towards sharper definition. Once, a Sikh was simply
a devotee of the Gurus. By 1925, it was felt that there was a need
to stress three features in the act of affirmation, namely belief in
the Ten Gurus, the Guru Granth Sahib, and the exclusive
statement of having no other religion. Behind this requirement
lay the awareness that some Sikhs described themselves as
Nanak panthis, that is devotees of Guru Nanak who rejected the
developments associated with Guru Gobind Singh embodied in
the Khalsa tradition. Secondly, there was also a tendency among
some Sikhs to value some of the hymns of the Guru Granth Sahib
more than others. For example, chamars, members of the leather
worker jati, honoured Ravidas, Sangats comprised solely of
chamars might use only his compositions. They also came to
regard Ravidas as a guru, a status denied him by Sikhs. The
reference to Ten Gurus could be applied against this tendency.
Thirdly, while Sikhs at the popular level of their religion may
declare themselves to be Sikhs and Hindus or even Sikhs and
Christians, the condition of the Panth at the turn of the century
required the inclusion of the phrase 'no other religion' when the
opportunity came to use it.

A proposal for an Act to place all the Gurdwaras of India under
the control of one body is being considered at the time of
writing. It will be interesting to see how it defines a Sikh.

Ravidasis

Mention has already been made of Ravidasis, people who belong
to the same social group as the mystic Ravidas (cc1414–cc1526).
They tried to improve their untouchable status by becoming
Sikhs who were considered to be egalitarian and included
compositions of Ravidas in their scriptures. The attempt was not
successful, as was the effort which some made to improve their
lot through conversion to Christianity. They were permitted to
participate in the religious life of the Panth but usually not to

serve on committees. Sikhs of other social groups would not intermarry with them. They have responded by establishing their own religious institutions, though they keep the Sikh outward form and use the Guru Granth Sahib as the focus of their worship. Often they now prefer to call their place of worship a sabha (association) rather than gurdwara. An edition of the works of Ravidas is being prepared which may replace the Guru Granth Sahib in worship.

Valmikis

Equally unfortunate is the story of chuhra, (sweeper/cleaner caste) experience. This untouchable group found its attempt to gain full acceptance within the Panth equally difficult. It has therefore turned from Sikhism and Christianity to Valmiki (sometimes written as Balmiki), the legendary author of the great Hindu epic, the Ramayana, recognized him as their founder guru and installed the Ramayana as their worship focus, sometimes together with the Guru Granth Sahib. However, they tend no longer to keep the uncut hair and turban and seem closer now to Hinduism than Sikhism, though they would insist, like the Ravidasis on their distinctiveness, but their wish to remain in good standing with Sikhs as well as other religious groups. Like the Ravidasis their meeting places tend to be called sabhas, associations, rather than gurdwaras. A chuhra named Bhai Jaita Ranghreta recovered the head of Guru Tegh Bahadur in Delhi and brought it to his son, the tenth Guru. For this his family and caste were honoured. The Guru told him, 'Ranghretas are the Guru's own sons'. Pictures of this episode are often to be found in Valmiki sabhas but the existence of these buildings bear witness to the reality that the esteem in which the Guru held them is not shared today by the Sikh Panth generally.

The nineteenth century saw the emergence of two important Sikh reform movements led by Dayal Das (died 1855) and Baba Balak Singh (died 1861). Both of these remained within the Panth but produced a succession of their own gurus. It is against such groups that the emphasis upon 'Ten Gurus' in the Gurdwaras Acts of 1925 and 1971 was intended, and also the Radhasoamis. They also originated in the nineteenth century but outside Punjab, in Agra in 1861, and outside the Panth. They have never regarded the Guru Granth Sahib as their scripture as have the four groups previously mentioned.

However, some of their gurus have come from Sikh backgrounds and Sikhs in Punjab and elsewhere sometimes attend their gatherings at Beas, following common Indian practice of seeking spiritual guidance wherever it might be found. The constitution of the Singh Sabha gurdwara in Southall, UK, which says that members should 'reject belief in any other gurus' (than the ten Sikh), is specifically intended to discourage Sikhs from religious association with these groups whose danger lies in their apparent proximity to the beliefs and practices of the Panth as well as their physical presence in a very multi-religious conurbation. Unlike the Punjabi village it has no one group that can assert domination, especially as the context is one of a Britain in which the norms have changed only slightly from what they were 50 years ago. Whichever community gains local ascendancy it remains a fairly powerless minority subgroup in broader social terms.

In our conclusion to this discussion of a search for uniformity within the Panth, we must point to the Rahit Maryada's pervading emphasis upon the desirability that all Sikhs should become amritdhari. Although, as has been seen, the Gurdwaras Acts do not define 'Sikh' so rigidly, it is clearly perceived as the norm towards which all should strive. Pressure to accept this definition of orthodoxy is growing both in India and in parts of the Diaspora.

Khalistan

This is the name of a concept which some Sikhs hope will be realized in the establishment of an independent Sikh country based on the historical and geographical Punjab, not the present small north-west Indian state. The concept goes back beyond the Partition of India in 1947. In 1945, the Shromani Akali Dal (Sikh political party) put forward a scheme when it became clear that the British government accepted partition. This province would remain within the Indian Union.

Sikhs now tersely express their view of these events in the sentence, 'The Muslims got Pakistan, the Hindus got India, what did the Sikhs get?' Faced with the choice of belonging to India or Pakistan, Sikhs say, they chose India because Nehru offered them virtual autonomy whereas Jinnah had offered a religious freedom that he could not guarantee. He said, 'I see nothing wrong in an area and a set up in the North wherein the Sikhs can also experience the glow of freedom.

This promise has never become a reality. The federal India which Nehru and Gandhi envisaged, as well as Ambedkhar who drafted its Constitution, has never matched their ideal. It was to have been a secular nation, secular that is in the Indian sense of one in which all religions enjoyed equal respect and none was privileged. To protect the secular ideal against his great fear of communalism, Nehru deferred granting Sikh demands for a Punjab state defined along linguistic lines, a quite proper request within the Constitution. As a reward to Sikhs for their loyalty during the 1965 Indo-Pakistan war, his daughter, Indira Gandhi, who had become prime minister, granted it. The Punjabi Suba, as it was called, of 1966, however, did not satisfy the aspirations of those who wanted a Sikh state albeit within the Union. As Mrs Gandhi defended national unity, designated Kashmir, Assam and Punjab as the regions which threatened it, and increased the powers of central government, so opposition grew.

In Punjab it was led by Sant Jarnail Singh Bhindranwale whom the Congress party hoped to use to embarrass the dominant Sikh Akali Dal party. He proved to be his own man and was eventually destroyed in June 1984, only by an Indian army assault upon the Darbar Sahib complex which he had been obviously fortifying for at least six months. On 31 October Mrs Gandhi was assassinated by Sikh members of her bodyguard. In

figure 16 an overall view of the Harimandir Sahib in the Darbar Sahib complex which is set in the centre of a large rectangular artificial lake. Visitors always walk around the marble walkway (parkarma) in a clockwise direction

Delhi and elsewhere, Sikhs were attacked and many were killed. Rajiv Gandhi, who replaced his mother as premier, attempted to solve the Punjab crisis by drawing up the Punjab Accord with a Sikh leader, Sant Harchand Singh Longawal, in July 1985, but he lacked the authority to implement the agreement. On 26 January 1986, for example, Chandigarh was to be transferred to Punjab. The day came and went but nothing happened. Longawal himself was killed by Sikh militants.

The Punjab crisis remains unresolved. Most Sikhs recognize that their future lies within the Indian Union, but in a modified federation in which central authority is curbed and cannot be imposed upon the regions in the way that Mrs Gandhi did. A growing number of Sikhs, however, do no believe that an Indian government will ever have the will to relinquish central power and the immense patrimony which goes with it. At present the militants may seem to be checked in Punjab, though still active. Outside India, the Council of Khalistan under its President, Dr Gurmit Singh Aulakh, (based in Washington) seeks to influence the USA, with some success and other governments, and draw attention through such organizations as Amnesty International and the United Nations to what they describe as the continued repression of the Sikh nation. Some Diaspora Sikhs support the Khalistan movement financially, many regard the cause as futile, but few, in Britain at least, would not denounce separatist demands openly for they might be dubbed disloyal to their religion.

In 1991, the Bharatiya Janata Party (BJP) won many seats in India's general election. These were gained by a clear religious appeal to Hindus to make India a Hindu nation. This has often been accompanied by criticisms of Christians and Muslims for being aliens, not true Indians. Sikhs are fearful of the rise of Hindu militancy for two reasons. If the Hindus tell them that they are really Hindus (as the Vishnu Hindu Parishad, a Hindu religious and political group, suggests, calling them 'Keshdhari Hindus') their distinctive identity is threatened. If churches and mosques are attacked they fear that gurdwaras will be the next chosen targets. Some Sikhs have moved to the Punjab from other parts of India, anxious to avoid this danger. Occasional Sikh attacks on Hindus in Punjab should be seen in the context of creating an exclusively Sikh state *de facto* by forcing Hindus to flee, if the Hindu government, as they see it, will not grant them one *de jure*. This is a form of ethnic cleansing. In every respect it goes against the teachings of the Gurus.

The solution of the Punjab problem may lie in a radical redrafting of the Indian Constitution to produce a federation that gives more regional autonomy. Punjab is not the only region to have been in conflict with the centre, but it is the only one in which religion and politics have united to create a powerful opposition. The rise of Hindu political parties, such as the BJP and the Rashtriya Swayamsevak Sangh (RSS) with their communalist appeal to Hindus, arguing that tolerance of non-Hindus in the land of Hinduism has gone too far, is unlikely to bring such federal reform nearer, unless the Congress government can find leaders of the stature of Mahatma Gandhi and Nehru to reinforce the secular democratic ideals upon which India was founded.

15

Sikh attitudes to other religions

In this chapter you will learn:

- the notion of critical universalism
- the attitudes of the Gurus to other religions
- the influence of history.

India is a land of many faiths. In most parts of the country they may all be experienced as one goes along the main highways. The vast majority of the population of about 1 billion people is Hindu, they number about 800 million, but Islam has 180 million adherents – a population only paralleled by Indonesia and Pakistan. Other groups are fairly regionally concentrated though members are to be found in almost every state; Jains mainly in Rajasthan, Sikhs in Punjab and Haryana, Christians in Kerala. There are now few Jews; Buddhists come usually from the dalit sections of the nation, descendants of the followers of Dr Ambhedkar who discovered that the new India of the late 1940s could not give them the equality to which they aspired. In Guru Nanak's day there were no Buddhists in India, and Christians had not spread beyond the south.

It is possible, of course, not to be affected in any way by contact with members of other religions. This position can be found even among people active in the interfaith movement. 'Live and let live', 'we all worship the same God' are the slogans, while a critical awareness of beliefs other than one's own does not seem desirable or necessary. It is possible for academics too to adopt this kind of position, bracketing out one's own beliefs in the study of others. One may also encounter believers who deny the validity of other creeds as a matter of dogma, and so do not find any need to study them, much less share in discussions about them.

Guru Nanak himself pays much attention to the religious traditions that he encountered, principally forms of Hinduism and Islam. To understand Sikhism fully it is necessary to be conversant with his response to them; any study of Sikh attitudes to other religions must begin with Guru Nanak.

A few general points must be made before turning to details. First, it was common until very recently to describe Sikhism as syncretistic, a blend of Hinduism and Islam. Sometimes writers asserted that the Guru took the best from the two religions! We must ask what constitutes the best, what criteria of choice can be used. His affirmation of one God might be seen as Islamic, his attitude to women might be said to accord with some forms of Hindu bhakti, but with a greater study of these facets, it will be recognized that though his monotheism may be similar to that of some Sufis, an Islamic origin does not seem satisfactory. As for the equality of women and men he seems to go well beyond the norms of his day, and we have not addressed such issues as ritual pollution or the divisions in society which are to be found in Islam as well as in the Hindu caste system (see page 24). Sikhism must be studied ultimately sui generis and recognized to be a distinctive revealed religion or success will not be achieved. As with all other features of his life and work, the basis of Guru Nanak's attitudes to the religions he encountered is his concept of God and humanity.

Guru Nanak often affirmed that he had but one guru, God, the Sat Guru or Guru of Gurus. He had no human spiritual preceptor. Suggestions that he was a disciple of Kabir are based on unreliable sources.

Besides the belief that God is one, Guru Nanak taught that God had no garb, that is no form or attachments by which one could claim deity to be Hindu or Muslim. He used Hari, Ram and Gopal, Allah, Khuda and Sahib, (e.g. AG 903), depending on the beliefs of his hearers, but his fundamental affirmation was that:

> *My master is one, brother, the One who alone exists*
> *(AG 350)*

Guru Nanak was what might be described as a critical universalist, though taken to its logical limits, he might, perhaps, be said to hold a position which transcends accepting the authenticity or validity of all religions, for each, at some point, implies that the Truth is limited by or conditioned by its own tenets.

He was not hesitant in challenging ideas, beliefs, or practices that fell short of the vision that he had received summed up in the belief in one God and one humanity.

The concepts of ritual purity and pollution have already been discussed (page 24). No further comment on them need be made here.

Priestly domination of one group of people by another was also anathema. Sometimes Guru Nanak criticized the potential for exploitation that resulted from religious power, whether it be of the Brahmin, yogi, or mullah. More fundamentally, he believed that the Nam-filled devotee, the gurmukh, had no need of the offices of such ministers or of intermediaries of any sort. Guru Nanak often spoke of the necessity of having a guru, but in doing so he was never commending himself but the Sat Guru, God (see page 130–1).

> *What power have I to utter the name of God? If you*
> *cause me to worship then only I can worship. If you*

abide within me, then I am rid of ego. Whom else
should I serve? Without you there is no other.
(AG 1331)

As a married young man Nanak went to Sultanpur to live with
his older sister, Nanaki. There, his brother-in-law, Jai Ram,
found him employment as an accountant in his Muslim master's
employment (page 21). One of the first stories relating him to
Islam belongs to this period.

One day soon after his river Bein experience, Nanak was at the
home of Daulat Khan Lodi having a religious discussion with him
and the village qazi. The subject was Guru Nanak's assertion that
there is neither Hindu nor Muslim (see page 21). The time came
for the second prayer. According to one version the Guru
committed the grave insult of laughing during the prayer, others
simply say that while the qazi and the headman prayed he stood
in silence. Asked to defend his behaviour the Guru replied saying
that he could not have prayed because they were not praying. The
qazi, he said, was anxious because his young filly had been left
untethered in the courtyard behind the house. A well was there
and he feared that the horse might fall into it. As for the Khan,
his servants were in Kabul trading in horse, he was wondering
what kind of profit they had made. Niyat, intention, is often said
to be the most important requirement in Islamic prayer. Neither
of them had the right intention so, Guru Nanak said, they were
not actually praying. He could not then, pray with them.
Frequently, such anecdotes are followed by a spiritual message.
On this occasion he declared:

> *There are five prayers, they have five names. The first*
> *is truthfulness, the second honest learning, the third*
> *charity in God's name, the fourth purity of intent, and*
> *the fifth God's admiration and praise. Repeat the*
> *kalima of good deeds [the statement that 'There is no*
> *God but God and Muhammad is his prophet'], then*
> *call yourself a prophet. (AG 141)*

This account is a denunciation of hypocrisy, deceit and formal-
ism. It is clearly not a rejection of Islamic worship as such. Of
Allah he said:

> *Baba Allah is inscrutable. He is boundless. His abode*
> *is holy and so are his names. He is the True Sustainer.*
> *His will surpasses comprehension. It cannot be*
> *described adequately. Not even a hundred poets*

assembled together could describe the smallest part of it. All hear and talk about him, none fully appreciates his worth. *(AG 141)*

Allah consults no one when he makes or unmakes, gives or takes away. He alone knows his decree *[qudrat],* he alone is the doer. He beholds everyone and bestows grace on whom he wills. *(AG 53)*

These sentences might well have been uttered by a Muslim.

Guru Nanak could even find some place for the varna system and much more for the Vedas. He does not reject the Hindu varna structure, and certainly not the authenticity of the Vedas as the following passages demonstrate:

The way of union is the way of divine knowledge. With the brahmin the way is through the Vedas, the kshatriyas way is that of bravery. That of the shudra is the service of others. The duty of all is meditation on the One. *(AG 1353)*

Here the emphasis is not on purity but on service, the cardinal Sikh virtue.

The Vedas preach the sermon of devotional service. He who continually hears and believes sees the Divine Light. The shastras and smirtis impress meditation on the Name. *(AG 731 and 832)*

Hearing alone is not enough. Responding through faith is what matters:

A fool residing with a pandit hears the Vedas and shastras. Like a dog with a crooked tail he remains unchanged. *(AG 990)*

Beyond the Vedas is its creator who must be attained if liberation is to be achieved:

It is God who created the Vedas. It is through the One that the world is saved. *(AG 930)*

One is led to the conclusion that Guru Nanak's primary belief in the immediacy of brahma vidya, the liberating knowledge of Brahman, meant that belief systems held a subordinate place in his theology. It does appear, however, that through aspects of them, such as imbibing the vedic message or sincerely performing namaaz God could be realized. We may not agree that conventional Hindu belief and Islam were fundamentally wrong (McLeod 161). Truth could be reached through them, though it may be said to lie beyond them.

Jainism

Before ending this section on Guru Nanak's attitudes to other religions some mention might be made of the Jains. He only refers to them twice in any detail. They have never been a numerically large, popular Indian way of liberation. The Jain movement is, in a sense, one with the upanishads and Buddhism, but unlike the former, and in common with the way of the Buddha, it was regarded as unorthodox because it did not acknowledge the authority of the Vedas. It owes its origins to Mahavira, the twenty-fourth Tirthankara or teacher, who may have lived at about the same time as the Buddha, some writers suggest 599 to 526 BCE. Jainism is extremely austere and ethical in its teachings and requirements. The laity must take three vows – of non-violence, truthfulness and charity. This means that Jains are vegetarian, concerned for the environment, and have often practised as businessmen, such is their honesty. Such an austere religion has never appealed to the masses and today may have less than 4 million adherents.

Jains do not believe in a personal creator God. Liberation is through their way of life and entails becoming a monk or nun, which may not be achieved in their present existence. It is non-theistic, the gods are themselves souls on the way to liberation. The religion is also dualistic with a division into that which is alive (jiva), and non-living (ajiva). Among the ajiva is karma, which attaches itself to the jiva and weighs it down, thus preventing the attainment of moksha, of mukti, to use the Sikh term. Jains were known to be in Lahore in the time of the Emperor Akbar and may have been found in the Punjab in Guru Nanak's day. He certainly considered them deserving of attention.

> They pluck the hairs from their heads, drink water in which people have washed, and beg leftovers. They rake up their excreta and inhale its smell. They detest water. They pluck their heads like sheep and smear their hands with ashes. They turn from living with their parents and families, leaving them to grieve. No rice balls are offered to the ancestors and funeral rites

are neglected. No lamps are lit for them. They do not seek the refuge of the sixty-eight places of pilgrimage or feed Brahmins. They always remain filthy, day and night, and there is no tilak to be seen on their foreheads. They sit about in groups as if in mourning, and do not share in public activities. Brush in hand, begging bowl over the shoulder, they walk along in single file.

From water came the jewels when Mount Meru churned the ocean. The gods established sixty-eight pilgrimage places where festivals are held and God is praised. The wise always walk. Muslims pray after ablutions, after bathing. Hindus worship. Water is poured on the living and dead to purify them.
Nanak says, these pluck haired devils will have none of this.

Rain brings happiness. The cow can graze continually and the housewife churns the curds. With the ghee, havan, puja and festivals are sanctified. The Guru's the ocean all his teachings are the rivers, bathing in them brings glory.
If the pluck haired do not bathe, says Nanak, let seven hands full of ashes be put on their heads. (AG 149/150)

The second passage reads:

Some are Jains who wander in the wilderness. They are wasted away by the Primal Being. The Name is not on their lips and they do not bathe in places of pilgrimage. They pluck their heads with their hands, refusing to use a razor. Night and day they remain filthy. They have no time for social behaviour or responsibility. They live in vain.

Their minds are soiled and impure. They eat one another's left overs. Without the Name and virtuous living, no one is ever blessed. By the Guru's grace the mortal merges in the One reality. (AG 1285)

One must say at the outset of discussing these passages that Jains would certainly deny their veracity and be concerned about what they would see as the pillorying of their beliefs and practices. Today, they are among the most respected communities in Indian society.

The vitriolic attack on Jains is in sharp contradiction to the portraits one is accustomed to of a benign, white bearded old man. Though this picture may be as far from the truth as popular notions of the God of the Bible who has a long white beard and sits enthroned on a cloud! Why Guru Nanak made it is not the only perplexing matter. In fact the question 'why' may be the easiest to answer.

Ishnan features strongly in Guru Nanak's teaching, together with *Nam*, meditation, and *Dan*, giving to the needy. It means washing or bathing. It seems a little strange for the emphasis to be upon an apparent ritual when this aspect of religious behaviour is so frequently under attack. Ishnan, however, for Sikhs, has to do with cleanliness and hygiene rather than ritual. Each morning most of the people of India, regardless of faith, bathe. This is often a preliminary to puja or, in the case of Sikhs, Nam Simran, but it is a practice of which the Guru approved (the river Bein episode began with Guru Nanak bathing), and which he encouraged or even demanded of his disciples. At the other extreme come the Jains who, according to the Guru, rejoice in filth.

Jains are also non-theistic in practice. As we have noted the gods are beings who are themselves on the journey to enlightenment. Guru Nanak believed emphatically in one God who was essential to spiritual liberation. They were engaged in a vain journey.

It is also asserted that Jains fail to give alms and reject their living families and their ancestors. They are clearly indifferent to society and lack community responsibility, Dan, the practice of alms giving and mutual support, which Guru Nanak considered to be so important. In common with other groups they denied the value of the householder life, which he saw as the cornerstone of society and the means by which men and women achieved spiritual liberation.

What is more difficult to comprehend is the Guru's apparent approval of Hindu practices, which he elsewhere condemns, such as making pilgrimages or feeding Brahmins. Perhaps we may infer that he was not praising these activities but was really demonstrating how the Jains fell even below the expressions of Hindu devotion. There may be a chance that Hindus will experience God through the acts they undertake, the Jains have no hope, they are 'rejected by God'.

Plucking the hair on the head has drawn some comments from Sikhs who have seen in it an assertion that people should keep the natural form which they were given. This is a reason why

Khalsa Sikhs, and many others, though not all, keep the kesh intact neither shaving nor cutting their hair. (One has even heard of Sikhs being greatly exercised in their consciences if surgery requires the removal of body hair.)

There is, however, a couple of lines in which Jains are treated more positively. Digambara is the name by which the group who went about naked are known. The Guru writes, with ahimsa in mind, the Jain tradition of not injuring sentient beings, or, to put it positively, reverence for life, a principle that greatly attracted Mahatma Gandhi:

> The naked Digambara is one who has compassion and examines his inner self. He slays his own self and does not slay others. You are but One, though your appearances are many. (AG 356)

This occurs in a passage where yogis, Jains and other practitioners of austerities are commended if the emphasis is placed upon trust in God.

An explanation of Guru Nanak's responses to the forms of religion he encountered

From the above examples it seems impossible to provide a simple answer to the question of what Guru Nanak thought of the forms of religion he encountered. Certainly much that he saw met with his disapproval but he could find a place for the Vedas and for Islamic practices and beliefs.

A clue to his views might be found in his attitudes to Jains and Naths. For these he had little time or none. The unimportance of God which they seem to have preached by their conduct and their words was in stark contradiction to a teacher whose message had God at its very heart.

His monotheism left no place for apparent polytheism. We know that a fundamental Hindu teaching is that God is one:

> Truth is One; sages call it by many names such as Indra, Mitra, Varuna, Yama, Garutman, or Matarishvan. (Rig Veda: 1:164:46)

The Yajur Veda, another important scripture, expresses the same truth as follows:

For an awakened soul, Indra, Varuna, Agni, Yama,
Aditya, Chandra, – all these names represent only
One spiritual being. (32:1)

These words lie at the heart of the religion but for many devotees
and non-Hindu observers the reality seems to be polytheistic.
The pictures and images which may be seen in a mandir, ranging
from Rama and Hanuman, to Jesus, the Virgin Mary, Guru
Nanak and Gandhi, might convey this message to the
uninformed, rather than one of diversity within unity which is at
the heart of Hinduism. Certainly that seems to have been true of
the village Hinduism that Guru Nanak experienced.

Duality, which popular, polytheistic Hinduism, seemed to teach,
was something else abhorrent to the Guru. Therefore rival
religious systems would be inimical, not only the sectarian
differences within Hinduism but also the discord that Islam
might be creating in villages and regions that had once been
Hindu. Social duality included caste and for its distinctions he
again had nothing but disapproval. The equality of man and
woman would also come under this heading.

An ethic, or lack of it, which did not emphasize social responsibility was also anathema. Thus the Jains were sharply rebuked
but again caste, which could express concern for members of
one's own biradari but ignored others who were outside it,
would be a target for his comments.

Finally, we are again left with the phrase Nam, Dan and Ishnan.
At Kartarpur we may envisage a community focused upon these
three principles of meditation upon the One, care for everyone
regardless of gender, caste, wealth, or beliefs, and cleanliness. To
quote Bhai Gurdas, the great Sikh theologian who lived in the
century after Guru Nanak:

> *The sun with its light dispels the darkness of night.*
> *Likewise the gurmukh, making people understand the*
> *importance of Nam, Dan, and Ishnan, sets them free*
> *from the bondage (of transmigration).*
> *(Var 16: Pauri 7)*

Guru Arjan

The fifth Guru exercised a considerable influence upon Sikh
attitudes to other religions both directly and indirectly. He was
responsible for a consolidation of the Panth as an entity distinct

from Hinduism and Islam. This he did principally by compiling a scripture, the Adi Granth (see Chapter 12). Like Hindus and Muslims the Sikhs now had a Book for which they claimed divine authority. The word 'adi', as mentioned above (page 116), means first in the cardinal sense of primal or primary. ('Pehle' is usually used of the first of a sequence.) Adi Guru is a term frequently used to describe the original guru of a particular order. Caitanya, as adi guru is revered even more highly than Krishna by his devotees.

Inclusion of bhagat bani in the Adi Granth has already been noted (p.112). It is highly relevant to our examination of Sikh attitudes to other faiths for it is, perhaps, the only example of a corpus of literature not of the particular religion being included in its scripture. (The inclusion of the Jewish scriptures in the Christian Bible is not comparable or relevant here). It is an indication of the critical universalism of Sikh thought; critical in that only material which accorded with the Gurus' concepts of God and humanity were admitted; universalist in that compositions by Hindus of a variety of varnas, and those of Muslims were included. Importantly, nothing already in the Qur'an or sruti or smirti was incorporated. Synthesis or synchronism was evidentially not in the fifth Guru's mind any more than it had been in Guru Nanak's, there may have been a suggestion that here was a scripture open to all. Certainly Sikhs in the present day make much of the bhagat bani as an example of ecumenical openness.

The scripture was installed in the Harimandir Sahib and here again openness is symbolized. Unlike a mandir it had four entrances indicating that members of all four varnas might worship in it. By extension, in modern times it has become common to extend the symbolism to include people from the four corners of the earth. Sikhs also cherish a tradition that a Qadarite Sufi, Mian Mir, laid the foundation stone, though many Sikh historians question this whilst acknowledging that he was probably present on the occasion.

Whether anything can be made of Guru Arjan's aspirations for his son, Hargobind, is a matter of conjecture. The name means 'world lord', and when the child was born, late in the Guru's life by Indian standards, he was 32, he declared:

> *The Sat Guru has sent the child. The long-lived child has been born by destiny. When he came and acquired an abode his mother's heart rejoiced greatly. The son,*

the saint of the world ruler lord (Gobind) is born. The
primal writ has become manifest amongst all. In the
tenth month by divine command, the baby has been
born.
Sorrow has departed and great joy become manifest.
The Sikhs sing the gurbani in their joy. (AG 396)

Sikh confidence and self-esteem was high, as the above passage
demonstrates. The Panth was large enough and wealthy enough
for rivals to covet the gaddi. In part Hargobind's birth was
welcome as a means of thwarting such ambitions. At this time
the Mughal ruler Akbar the Great was viewing all religions
benignly. Jesuits were present at this court and had some hopes
of Guru Arjan's conversion while Muslim courtiers and theologians were dismayed by his respectful tolerance, which extended
to being married to a Hindu princess. Soon after the Adi Granth
had been compiled enemies of the Guru told the Emperor that it
contained material blasphemous to Islam. He asked to see a copy
and one was dispatched to him under the care of Bhai Buddha
and Bhai Gurdas. Portions were read, of which Akbar approved,
giving money towards costs incurred in producing it, and saying
that he would visit the Guru on his return from Lahore. After
enjoying the Guru's hospitality he acceded to his request that the
taxes of Punjab should be revoked for one year to offset the
effects of a serious famine. It may be that Guru Arjan hoped that
his might be the religion to provide the Emperor with the
alternative to Hinduism and Islam for which he was searching
through his monotheistic syncretism known as 'The Divine
Faith'.

Guru Arjan also stated, however:

I do not keep the fast [vrat] or observe Ramadan. I
serve only the One who will save me in the end. The
One World ruler is my God who ministers justice to
both Hindus and Muslims. I do not go on hajj to the
Ka'ba or worship at tiraths. My body and soul belong
to the One and no other. I do not perform puja or
namaaz. Taking the formless One in my mind I make
obeisance there to God. I am neither a Hindu nor a
Muslim. My body and soul belong to the One called
Allah by Muslims and Ram by Hindus. (AG 1136)

This is not to be regarded as a denial of the authenticity of either
of the major religions but a proclamation of a God who
transcends them both.

Whatever Guru Arjan's hopes, they were dashed only two years after his meeting with Akbar. The Emperor died and Guru Arjan was accused of taking the side of the loser, prince Khusrau in the war of succession won by Jehangir. The Guru was tortured and died in 1606, becoming the first Sikh martyr.

This event made the Panth reassess its relationship with the Mughals and its self-understanding. There is a Sikh tradition that Guru Arjan told his son that when he mounted the gaddi of guruship he should wear two swords, those of miri and piri, signifying temporal and spiritual authority. The confidence that had been part of the Sikh psyche only a few years before was challenged and trust between the Panth and government never fully recovered.

Guru Tegh Bahadur and Guru Gobind Singh

1675 was the occasion of an even more devastating and significant event, the execution of the ninth Guru, the grandson of Guru Arjan. It is regarded by Sikhs as unequivocally an act of religious persecution. A group of Kashmiri pandits looking for help against the aggressive attempts to convert them by the Emperor Aurangzeb, came to him. At the suggestion of the Guru's young son, he went to Delhi with a small group of followers where they were arrested. They were offered the choice of conversion or death. Preferring the latter they were executed, the Guru last. A gurdwara stands on the site in Chandi Chowk. Some words by Guru Gobind Singh, the son who had encouraged Tegh Bahadur to take up the Hindus' cause:

> For their frontal mark and their sacred thread he wrought a great deed in the age of Darkness. This he did for the sake of the pious, silently giving his head.

From this time 'Mughal' is replaced by 'Muslim' in the vocabulary of persecution. But even now the story does not become one of unrelenting Sikh-Muslim hostility. In fact Guru Gobind Singh was campaigning with Aurangzeb's successor Bahadur Shah in 1708 when he received a mortal blow from an assassin.

He exemplified the beliefs of his predecessors in saying:

> Salute him who is without the label of a religion.

More fully, in a composition known as 'Akal Ustad' the tenth
Guru wrote:

> *Hindus and Muslims are one. The same Being is*
> *creator and nourisher of all. Recognise no distinction*
> *between them. Puja and namaaz are the same. All*
> *people are one, it is through error that they appear*
> *different. . . . Allah and Abhek are the same, the*
> *Puranas and Qur'an are the same. They are all*
> *creations of the One.*

The eighteenth century

Sikhs often present the century as a continuous armed struggle
for survival when, for much of the time a price was put on the
heads of Sikhs. Paintings in gurdwaras often depict this
graphically, the heads of decapitated Sikhs being carried on the
heads of spears, and famous martyrs dying heroically. These
undoubtedly still influence the attitudes of young Sikhs in the
twenty-first century but at the time lasting harm may not have
been done to Sikh-Muslim relations, however, because of an
event that took place at the very end of the period.

In the nineteenth century the Sikh Empire was established under
Maharajah Ranjit Singh, who captured Lahore in 1799. It only
came to an end as the result of two wars with the British after his
death in 1839 and their annexation of the Punjab in 1849. During
this period Muslims served in the imperial administration and
relationships generally seem to have been lastingly amicable.
Elderly Sikhs, born as late as the 1930s, still talk of learning and
speaking Urdu and of villages in which the religions existed
harmoniously. Many Sikhs regard the Sikh Empire as a fore-
runner of the secular state established by Nehru in 1947.

It is significant that one of the reasons given by Sikhs for not
participating in the Mutiny or First War of Independence in
1857 is that they had no desire to see a Mughal Empire restored
as the result of success!

Independent India

Towards the end of the nineteenth century Sikhs were alarmed by
the missionary zeal of two groups, Christian and Hindu in the
form of the Arya Samaj. The latter did not meet with great success

because its founder, Dayananda Sarasvati, displayed a scornful attitude towards Guru Nanak and Sikh scriptures. Sikhs perceived the danger posed by these sophisticated challenges and responded through the Singh Sabha movement, which, from 1873, established educational institutions and generally encouraged learning. There was a flourishing of Sikh intellectual and cultural activity. Though one of the most important products of this resurgence was Bhai Kahan Singh Nabha's 'Hum Hindu Nahi' ('We are not Hindus'). As the twentieth century opened opposition became principally directed at the British Raj.

Partition and its aftermath

In 1947 came the Partition of India. The Sikhs opted to live in secular India rather than join the Islamic state of Pakistan. The Punjab was divided between the two. Lahore, the capital city of the nineteenth century Empire became part of Pakistan, as did Guru Nanak's birthplace, Talwandi. This time there was outright warfare and although historians may distinguish between Mughal and Muslim in the seventeenth and eighteenth century conflicts, it was now a struggle between religions. Punjabi villages can still be seen in which the mosque has become a fodder store and mounds of earth show where Muslim inhabitants were buried after being killed. There is no need to pursue this topic further other than to warn readers that they may encounter Sikh-Muslim hostility even though they have been told that Sikhs are friends with everyone. A few years ago an interfaith group planned a meeting on Sikhism, they were advised that no Muslims would attend but did not take the comment seriously – came the day, no Muslims were in the audience. Nowadays the religions may enjoy better relationships in diaspora communities, perhaps less so in India, and occasionally Pakistan which has no longer a Sikh population other than those caring for Sikh shrines. Sikh pilgrims to the shrines have not always been welcomed with traditional hospitality, however, it should be stated that this has often been when India and Pakistan have been at war. At the time of writing Sikhs report well cared for gurdwaras and freedom of access.

Operation Blue Star 1984

Hindu–Sikh relationships have generally been good. There is a saying: 'Hindu–Sikh bhai bhai', 'Hindus and Sikhs are brothers'.

Sometimes part of a family will be Sikh while other members are Hindu. In the diaspora it has become common to see Sikhs worshipping in a mandir especially where there is no local gurdwara. They also share some celebrations, such as Divali and though they may interpret them differently, at the level of celebration they may unite. During the events leading up to and after Operation Blue Star, in which the Indian army stormed the Darbar Sahib in 1984, there was considerable and often violent animosity between the two communities. Some of this has been consigned to history but the policy of militant Hindus, Hindutva, and other attempts to make India a more Hindu state perpetuate anxiety. No one should doubt how terrible and lastingly significant for the collective Sikh memory and the Panth's psyche this event was. Worldwide celebrations of the tercentenary of the Khalsa in 1999, including a major event at the Albert Hall and an exhibition at the Victoria and Albert Museum, which travelled to other cities worldwide, can disguise this. At the moment events are being planned to commemorate the compilation of the Adi Granth in 1604. To the extent that they will necessarily be associated with the Darbar Sahib they will rekindle pain if not animosity and distrust.

The new Nanakshahi Calendar which relates significant Sikh celebrations to the solar calendar instead of the Hindu Bikrami/Samvat era is not intended to distance Sikhs from Hindus (the principal melas will continue to be observed on the traditional occasions), but some people may regard it as a statement of Sikh distinction from Hinduism.

Sikhs actively participate in many inter-religious activities and, for example, have been present as observers at recent gatherings of the World Council of Churches. They do find it difficult, however, when they hear Jews, Christians and Muslims, describing themselves as the 'three monotheistic religions'. By now, readers of this book should be aware that no religion can claim to be more monotheistic than that founded by Guru Nanak!

As for the future one can only speculate but it is clear that Sikhs will remain faithful to the critical universalism of the Gurus while the historical and social context in which they live is likely also to be influential.

16

the Sikh dispersion

In this chapter you will learn:

- the story of Sikh migration
- reasons for migration
- the possible future of the Panth.

A story that Sikhs never tire of telling is that of Neil Armstrong when he landed on the moon. His pride at being first was soon dispelled when a taxi drew up and its Sikh driver asked him, 'Where to, sir?'!

Sikhism began in Punjab 500 years ago but that is not where it ends, even though that part of India is still the place that they regard as home.

Migration is one of the most important aspects of Sikhism in the last 150 years, especially the latter half of the twentieth century. Sikhs are now to be found in every English-speaking country and many others, particularly in Europe, South America, and the Gulf States where most are temporary contractual workers.

Sikhs were active in various parts of India before 1849 but it was after that year, when the British annexed Punjab, that the story of Sikh migration really began.

Another important date for Sikh migration beyond India was 1857, the year of the first independence struggle, known to British historians as the Mutiny. Sikhs stood aside from the uprising because they had no wish to reinstate the Mughals or any other Muslim rulers, and that seemed to them the likely consequence of its success. This won Sikhs favour with the British who began recruiting them into the army in increasingly large numbers. By 1870, Sikh soldiers were serving overseas. On retirement, after demobilization in India, they often returned to the colonies where they had been stationed, such as Malaya or Hong Kong, to become members of the police force or security guards for private companies. During the First World War, Sikhs fought at Gallipoli and other parts of Europe, as well as in Africa as part of the British army.

Sikh civilians also migrated. Sometime in the 1860s or 1870s individuals were working as camel drivers in Australia; usually they were described as Afghans, just as today they are sometimes called 'Pakis' in Britain and 'Iraqis' in the USA, especially during the Gulf Wars, by ignorant persons.

There was, however, migration by groups of Sikhs by the end of the century. Sometimes almost all the men of a village would go abroad, not to settle, but to make enough money to improve farms, businesses and family property back home. It would be interesting to know what motivated them to head for countries such as Australia or New Zealand, and how in those days they came to hear of prospects there for economic success.

Sikhs were especially prominent in the development of East Africa in the 1890s, helping to build the railways. They were Ramgarhias for the most part, a group mainly of *tarkhans* (carpenters), but including some blacksmiths, masons and bricklayers, the skills the British needed and the native Africans lacked. Rather than train the Africans, they encouraged Indians to migrate.

Other Sikhs went to California and Vancouver, as well as other areas of the Pacific region before the First World War. In 1902, Sikh soldiers from Hong Kong went to Canada to take part in celebrations marking the coronation of Edward VII. Some eventually returned as settlers to work in British Columbia's lumber mills. Sikhs were also to be found in California before the outbreak of the First World War.

Migration to Europe

The United Kingdom

The first known Sikh to arrive in Britain was Maharajah Dalip Singh, son of Ranjit Singh, the last ruler of the Sikh empire. After the empire was annexed in 1849, its 11-year-old ruler was placed in the custody of Sir John Login of the Bengal army, in whose care he converted to Christianity. Five years later Dalip Singh came to England, was received by Queen Victoria, and bought an estate in Elvedon, Suffolk. As time passed he became increasingly dissatisfied with his treatment and attempted to return to India, where he intended to be readmitted to the Sikh faith. He was stopped at Aden and returned to Europe, but not until he had taken amrit. In 1893, he died in Paris and was buried in Elvedon in Suffolk in the churchyard near his estate. So much attention has been given to Dalip Singh because in 1993, the centenary of his death, Sikhs planned pilgrimages and services and asked for a monument to be set up in Elvedon, to the consternation of its inhabitants. It has been reported that Anglican parishioners have wondered whether their church should be reconsecrated after a Sikh was found praying in it! For many years, the villagers have watched the visits of Sikhs with some anxiety.

Dalip Singh and Ram Singh, builder of the Indian rooms in Queen Victoria's Osborne House, were among a very few, but in their cases notable, Sikh visitors to Britain. In 1911, the first gurdwara in Britain was established in Putney with financial support from the Maharajah of Patiala, but others appeared only after the Second World War. Britain was apparently too far away for Sikh migrants and showed no sign of needing them as labour was sufficient and cheap enough. Nearby Ireland could meet all its labour needs. Sikh eyes were still on the Pacific region, which had already been pioneered and to which travel may have been easier.

Sikh and other Indian traders came to Britain between the wars. Many of them belonged to the Bhatra jati. They would arrive at a port, Bristol, Manchester, Cardiff or Portsmouth, for example, set up base in rented rooms, buy small domestic items such as brushes, cleaning cloths, shoelaces, perhaps culinary utensils, and go from door to door with their immense cases. Women might buy some items on credit and provide the salesman with a regular if hard-worked-for living. Other Sikhs might work in the open-air markets. None of these intended to settle. Their families remained in Punjab and the men returned to them when they had made enough money to go back to their villages with pride (izzat) and the ability to give their family some prosperity. Their success encouraged others, sometimes of different jatis, to take their chance.

Real settlement in Britain began in the late 1950s with an influx of economic migrants from Punjab, especially the Hoshiarpur district of the Jullundur doab, the area between the rivers Beas and Sutlej. They were augmented a decade later by families from East African countries which, having gained their independence, pursued policies of Africanisation. The British Sikh population now stands at 336,000, two thirds of whom were born in Britain. This is probably the largest Sikh population outside India, though American Sikhs might dispute the assertion. They have been heard to claim that the Sikhs in North America number 1 million. A book published in 1992 gives a population of only 9500 for the USA. The Canadian census of 1991 gave the number of Sikhs there as 147,400. Attempts to discover the numbers of members of any religion are notoriously difficult to make, unless a religious question is included in the national census, as it is in Australia, which had a population of 7795 Sikhs in 1991.

Britain's Sikhs as economic migrants chose to come to the United Kingdom because they were British, they had British passports, some were war veterans who had served in Europe, and during the boom years of the 1950s there was plenty of work. They went to the traditional industrial areas, West Yorkshire, Central Lancashire, the East and West Midlands and parts of London. Not many went to similar regions of Scotland, Wales, or Northern Ireland where there was still unemployment, or the mining areas of South Yorkshire or the North East where the coal industry was already shedding jobs. In brief, in common with all economic migrants through the centuries, they went where they were needed, not where they would compete with the existing labour force. They had little intention of staying permanently in the United Kingdom but legislation during the 1960s confronted them with the choice of bringing families to join them, or leaving Britain eventually to return to Punjab. The vast majority decided to stay and sent for their immediate relatives. They still maintain close ties with India, sending money to improve the family home or to build gurdwaras, dispensaries or schools. Their children, now grown-up and themselves parents, may visit Punjab less frequently. Many have never been to India and declare themselves to be British Sikhs, though experiences of racial discrimination and harassment make them uneasy about their status and future, so some move to what seems a more receptive North America. Events in India since 1984 remind them that Punjab is the Sikh homeland.

Sikhism is not a religion which looks for converts but a feature of the American diaspora is the large number of 'white', *gora*, Sikhs. In 1969 an Indian sant, or spiritual teacher, Harbhajan Singh Puri (Yogi Bhajan, to give him his popular name), began teaching *kundalini* yoga in the USA. Some of his students were attracted by his total lifestyle, which included vegetarianism as well as the usual amritdhari discipline, of daily nam simran (meditation upon the Sikh scriptures), the prohibition of alcohol, tobacco, drugs, and sex outside marriage, as well as his Sikh world view stressing equality and service. To these might be added his own strong and attractive personality. In November 1969, the first converts took amrit. Some doubts were expressed by Punjabi Sikhs when they saw gora Sikhs for the first time, dressed from head to foot in white Punjabi clothes and wearing turbans: both men and women, and their children. They have turned out, however, not to be hippies in transit from one fad to another, but serious Sikhs. Their children have been brought up in the Sikh way, some have even been educated at Sikh schools in India. The movement is sometimes known as 3HO, Healthy,

Holy and Happy, and by the end of 1975, 110 centres and 250,000 people were involved in its activities. Its preferred title is Sikh Dharma of the Western Hemisphere. It is also known as the Sikh Dharma Brotherhood. A declared aim of the sant and his followers is to revive Sikh commitment to Khalsa ideals in Western countries where they have often become neglected. The zeal of converts is proverbial as is the enthusiasm, and occasionally the arrogance, of youth. Punjabi attitudes to gora Sikhs have been mixed but they could have an important role to play in enabling the diaspora to distinguish universal Sikh values from those which are Punjabi.

Cultural changes among Sikhs in Britain

Some readers may have spent time living abroad. Unless they lived in an expatriate enclave, as some do by choice or others are compelled to do, they may have had to decide what to keep and what to discard of their native customs and traditions. Inside the home things need not change – until children begin to question the value of keeping the parental tongue in a strange land, or the Christmas tree and traditional meal – preferring to be like the people around them, especially their new peer group. Sikhs outside India find themselves facing the same kinds of challenges. Distinction between religion and culture tends to be a Western division unfamiliar and incomprehensible to many people of the East, though there are second- and third-generation settlers who are beginning to compartmentalize religious belief and practice and secular life at least to the extent of separating their understanding of the essence of Sikhism from a Punjabi/Indian lifestyle in respect of diet, dress, arranged marriages and language.

Language, however, is not a secular matter for observant Sikhs. The person who compares it with the child from England who goes to live in France, forgets English and causes pain in the family when he can no longer talk to grandma, has missed the point. There is, of course, this kind of distress, but Punjabi is, and will remain, the language of the Sikh religion. Neglect of language cuts Sikhs off from their spiritual heritage in the form of worship in the sangat and ability to understand the Guru Granth Sahib, as well as converse with family elders who are often custodians of the tradition at the popular level, transmitting it to their grandchildren. Those Sikhs who perceive this danger make a response that may take the form of reinforcing Punjabi culture, particularly in continuing to encourage arranged marriages between families which value the culture. The tendency to bring in a bride or groom from India is decreasing, not so much because of legal hurdles, but because of an awareness of changes in lifestyle among British Sikhs. The prospect of a partner from Punjab reinforcing parental values may be seen to pose a threat to the British bride or groom. This is not to say that arranged marriages in themselves are proving unacceptable. On the contrary, many young Sikhs appreciate the stability they can bring and recognize their advisability in a system where one is marrying into an extended family. It is the danger of marrying out that Sikhs most dread, yet there are many examples of this in America, especially on the west coast. What affinity with Sikhism will the children of these mixed marriages have? The answer depends on the attitude of both parents. Where the non-Sikh partner shares the life of the sangat as far as possible, even if they don't learn Punjabi, and the community is friendly and receptive, the evidence seems to point to children staying Sikh. When the Sikh spouse is indifferent to their heritage, the children end up in a kind of no man's land, prey to the valueless society which tends to surround them.

Changes in religious practice

We have already noted that Sikhs possess a strong sense of community. The Gurus spoke frequently of the sangat, the fellowship of believers, which was essential for spiritual and moral development. Guru Ram Das said:

> *Just as the poor castor oil plant imbibes the scent of the nearest sandalwood, so wrongdoers become emancipated through the company of the faithful.*
> *(AG 861)*

In Punjab, however, this does not necessarily mean regular congregational worship of the kind found every Sunday in Britain. Sikhs have no weekly holy day. They should go regularly to the gurdwara and remember God in paying their respects to the Guru Granth Sahib, but much of the daily prayer of devout Sikhs takes place in the home, meditating every morning and evening upon specified compositions found in the scripture. It is at gurpurbs, anniversaries of the birth or death of one of the Gurus, or at the festivals of Vaisakhi or Divali, when Sikhs are likely to gather as a religious community. In India in August, they will often travel to a place such as Bakale where Guru Tegh Bahadur was proclaimed Guru or to Goindwal in September to observe the anniversary of the death of Guru Amar Das.

Processions, known as *jalous*, or nagar kirtan, led by the Guru Granth Sahib and attendants are often a feature of such assemblies.

In the United Kingdom and elsewhere in the dispersion, the gurdwara has become the focus of Sikh life. Rooms in private houses were used by the first settlers, now warehouses, redundant churches or former schools have been converted into gurdwaras and many purpose-built ones have been constructed. There are now well over 100 British gurdwaras; in some cities, there may be as many as four. On Sundays, as the day convenient for Sikhs to meet, they are full. Weddings, held in the open or under marquees in India, take place in gurdwaras at weekends. The formal educational role of the gurdwara exceeds even its importance as a social centre where the elderly gather often for much of the day. Punjabi classes, training in playing the musical instruments used in worship, formal education in religion, all things unnecessary in Punjab, are essential functions of the British gurdwara.

Apparently a distinctive feature of Britain's community is the establishment of caste gurdwaras. Bhatras, a group ranked very low in the Hindu spectrum of caste, from which Sikhs, Christians and members of other religions derive their status, were the first Sikhs to come to Britain in any number. They established gurdwaras in the ports where they lived. A rented room provided them with a base to leave their belongings and some of their merchandise, which they carried in their heavy suitcases around the towns of the Welsh valleys or Yorkshire. Bhatras, it is said, were professional beggars. When they converted in large numbers to Sikhism they had to find another occupation. Sikhs should not beg. Therefore they became peddlars. The first post-war gurdwaras in Britain were established by Bhatras. When other Sikh groups eventually followed them, however, they preferred not to associate with such lowly Sikhs as soon as possible.

A majority of post-war Sikhs who came from Punjab were Jats, peasant landowners, though in Britain none of them has become a farmer. Socially, they despised not only Bhatras. Sometimes they lived uneasily with another group they regarded as inferior, Ramgarhias, whose occupational background was urban and industrial – owning garages, making and repairing machines, (often those used by Jats on their farms). The consequence has sometimes been separate Jat and Ramgarhia gurdwaras. Most Sikh settlers from East Africa, as has been mentioned, were Ramgarhias. Their skills had been invaluable in the development of the British colonies. When they came to Britain in the late 1960s and 1970s, more sophisticated in a Western sense and wealthier than migrants from India, they tended to associate with fellow Ramgarhias and to distance themselves from Jats. Religiously, however, all Sikhs can and do combine for important celebrations and to protest against matters, such as racial harassment, which do not discriminate between Sikh social groups. Elsewhere in the diaspora, caste gurdwaras do not seem to have developed. Sikhs from America are taken aback by the phenomenon and often express their disapproval of it. One can only speculate upon reasons for British eccentricity. One obvious explanation is the settlement of several zats in an area whereas in Punjab they might remain distinct, living in different villages. Another may be the actual numbers of Sikhs. Most United Kingdom cities have sufficient Ramgarhia or Jat Sikhs to make the financing of separate gurdwaras feasible. Clearly, Jats and Ramgharias have their own lifestyles which conflict. Perhaps the emergence of separate gurdwaras would be found in other countries if these two groups found themselves living side by side. Conclusions might only be possible, however, when a survey of zats in the USA (where it is claimed that there are now 300 gurdwaras) is carried out and compared with the British situation.

Well-endowed gurdwaras which can afford to do so often employ a granthi who conducts worship, naming ceremonies and weddings, and performs other functions on behalf of the sangat. This person, who can theoretically be male or female but is invariably male, may sometimes be described as a 'priest', but this only causes confusion. One of the main tenets of Sikhism is the rejection of the authority of the Vedas and of the brahmin caste as its interpreter and as a ritual mediator between humanity and God. Outside India, granthis often perform additional educational functions, teaching children to play the instruments used in worship or to read Punjabi, or deal with questions that their peers throw at them which never troubled their parents who grew up in Sikh homes, in a Sikh environment. Their effectiveness varies. Some are highly competent, fluent in English and experts in Sikhi, which knowledge of Sikhism is often called. Others possess only the basic skills required to conduct worship and ceremonies – the functions for which they were trained. So far, all granthis are Punjabi educated. There is no sign, as yet, of a college for granthis being set up in the West, though the need will increase as the cultural distance between Punjab and the dispersion increases.

Sants, like Harbhajan Singh, are important to Sikh life worldwide. They provide personal leadership and may become the focus of devotion, though they take care not to be seen as in any way rivalling the scripture's authority, or being regarded as gurus in the Hindu sense of the word. In India, a Sikh will go to a sant at his *dehra*, a settlement or encampment, which is the equivalent of a Hindu ashram. In the diaspora, sant gurdwaras have taken root. Some sants now spend much of their time travelling the world ministering to the needs of their devotees. They often teach their own particular interpretation of Sikhism, perhaps the importance of taking amrit initiation, of holding regular continuous readings of the Guru Granth Sahib, or of being vegetarian, or they may have a healing ministry.

Culture clashes in the diaspora

All male Sikhs are traditionally expected to wear the turban. For those who have been initiated it is essential, as is the kirpan. Some migrant Sikhs made the error of cutting their hair and abandoning the turban when they arrived from India, being assured by Sikhs already here that they would not find employment otherwise. They gradually became more confident and often discovered that the initial advice had been unsound so they readopted the turban and uncut hair. Some schools, transport authorities and other employers refused to recognize the right of Sikhs to wear the turban.

These disputes are normally resolved quickly. After all, Sikhs had worn turbans in the British army. The first clash with authority in Britain came in 1972 when Parliament legislated that crash helmets should be worn by motor cyclists. In 1976, Parliament passed the Motorcycle Crash Helmets (Religious Exemption) Act 'to exempt turban-wearing followers of the Sikh religion from the requirement to wear a crash helmet when riding a motorcycle'. Since then, the right to wear the turban has been generally accepted in all areas of British life. It is worn instead of a wig, for example, by a high court judge and, in accordance with an exemption granted in the Employment Act of 1989, instead of a hard-hat on some construction sites. The Sikh kirpan is recognized as having a ceremonial and defensive purpose, and to be an essential part of Sikh dress. Sikh responsibility has ensured that few people have questioned the right of Sikhs to wear it. Some years ago, the British Government signalled its intention of bringing in legislation to ban the carrying of knives. The Home Office assured Sikhs and Scots that their right to wear the kirpan and the skean dhu would be safeguarded. Less newsworthy has been a development relating to the use of Sikh names. It took some years for application forms to change 'Christian name' to 'forename' or 'given name', but even longer for some employers, especially the British Nursing Council (BNC), to accept that a Sikh woman's surname should be 'Kaur' and a man's 'Singh'. They insisted that a female nurse should register in her father's surname, otherwise she would be denied registration, even though she had passed all the necessary examinations. Since July 1983, the United Kingdom Central Council for Nursing, Midwifery and Health Visiting, which succeeded BNC as the registering authority, has adopted the policy of registering 'practitioners under the names which they would customarily use'. In some other European countries, Sikh converts have found it difficult or impossible to get their forenames recognized rather than those which are traditionally acceptable. Thus, a convert called Jean-Marie was only recently allowed to change his name to Darshan Singh on his French passport.

Sikhs in continental Europe

Britain has over 100 gurdwaras; in continental Europe Sikhs are few; there is only one gurdwara in France, six in Germany, one in the Netherlands and one each in Denmark, Norway and Sweden. These are converted houses or other buildings bought by Sikhs who have come from India or occasionally the United Kingdom, though there is now a purpose-built gurdwara in Frankfurt (Germany) and one in Italy.

Their location changes frequently as Sikhs move from one part of a country to another or even back to India or Britain. In Moscow, a Sikh student recently attended Guru Nanak gurpurb celebrations at the Indian Embassy and discovered groups of Sikhs gathering in one another's homes on Sundays to recite Sukhmani Sahib, pray and share langar. Such a meeting might one day lead to the founding of a gurdwara, or the Sikhs who attend it may move on. Europe's Sikh community outside Britain scarcely exists.

During 1993, there was some unrest in a district of Belgium to which Sikhs had gone to take part in harvesting as casual labourers. At times of high unemployment, there are always possibilities of non-whites being accused of job stealing. These often diminish when a group becomes established, meanwhile Sikhs are sometimes deterred from migrating to areas where none has been previously.

Sikhs in North America

The work of Sant Harbhajan Singh Yogi has already been mentioned as well as the fact that the estimated number of Sikhs in North America varies incredibly. Apart from some Sikhs who migrated almost a century ago to the British Columbia region of Canada and to California in the USA, most American Sikhs settled there after the Second World War. They took with them the skills that new areas of the economy needed, such as ability in scientific research, medicine, and technology. For the most part as much needed professionals, they have faced little discrimination in countries that are multicultural and pride themselves on being classless. The turban and uncut hair has caused some difficulties for Sikhs wishing to enter the US army, and in Canada in 1993 a branch of the British Colombia Legion prevented Sikh veterans entering a hall to join in Remembrance Day ceremonies because they were wearing turbans.

The impact of the dispersion will depend upon American Sikhs more than any other group. There are already several professorships and lectureships in Sikh studies held by Sikhs, whereas outside India opportunities to study Sikhism are limited, and there are Sikhs who are alert to issues facing Sikhs in the modern world. Attitudes to the ethical challenges mentioned elsewhere (Chapter 10) are among these, as is the need for young Sikhs to be able to practise their religion through the medium of English. As yet, many Sikhs, even in the USA, are understandably holding on to an insistence on the Punjabi language, arranged marriages and the keeping of the turban and uncut hair as preferred forms of defence against the alien and secular American culture, but others are trying to articulate a Sikhism which will be faithful to the message of the Gurus and capable of surviving and flourishing in the USA, and therefore the Western world, of the next century. Those American Sikhs whose children have married out appreciate the need for the non-Sikh partner and the children of the marriage to be able to feel comfortable within the Sikh faith. They see the need for translations of at least parts of the scriptures so that they can share the religion's spirituality.

Why did Sikhs migrate?

There are many answers to this question and it would be interesting for you to discover some yourself by talking to Sikhs when you have got to know them well enough to discuss personal matters. It is also important for anyone with the opportunity to record interviews with them or their children while the chance offers itself. In 1983, I returned from a research visit to India intending to do just this, but was only back in time for the funeral of the man I wanted to interview, Leeds' first Sikh. He was a Ramgharia, not a Bhatra, and came to the United Kingdom in 1938. When asked why he came, he replied that two men had returned to his village wearing gold watches and strange (Western) suits. When he asked his father where they had been he was told 'England'. His response was if they could do it so could he, and out he set!

Besides this kind of individual answer there are general ones which are offered.

- Famine. Sometimes writers mention famines in the nineteenth century, which forced Punjabis to migrate in order to survive.
- Membership of the British Indian army, which led to Sikhs literally discovering new horizons, and gave them secure pensions after their term of service. These were sufficient to keep them and their families, but not to establish businesses or landholdings. They returned to the countries in which they had been serving, where they knew gaps in employment existed.
- Lack of opportunities at home. Farms or businesses may only be able to find employment for a limited number of people, especially with mechanization. Surplus sons had to look elsewhere – and at the same time help the extended family to

prosper from their earnings so that they could eventually find a niche when they returned home.
- Lack of land. Most of Punjab had been cultivated by the late eighteenth century, when irrigation projects had become fully operational. Jats, especially, had to look elsewhere.
- Prospects abroad, like those offered to the craftsmen who went to East Africa.
- The affluence of Britain in the 1950s and opportunities which the British government and employers offered those willing to work unsociable hours. Advertisements informed Asians and people from the Caribbean of such work in textile mills and public transport.
- Demands for professional skills in countries like the USA or Indonesia. India cannot afford to employ all the graduates it produces.
- Sikh rejection of the concepts of ritual purity and pollution which stopped some Hindus migrating.

Why did families move?

It will be remembered that the usual pattern of migration was for males to go abroad and send money back to the home to which they would eventually return.

The chance to bring wives and children to join migrants seems to have been caused by two factors. One was the prospect of greatly improved living standards compared with the best that India could offer, including education, climate, and occupational opportunities for the next generation. The other was government policies. Fixed contracts do not lead to Sikhs trying to settle down with their families in Arab states. The choice of bringing dependants to Britain within a limited period early in the 1960s, or not at all, made Sikh men decide to stay in Britain and be joined by their families. On the other hand, changes in Australian laws in the 1970s enabled newly-arrived professional Sikh men to bring their families to join them and make migration to that country relatively easy for Sikhs today.

The future of Sikhs in the diaspora

It is, of course, impossible to make predictions in human affairs. Much depends on circumstances beyond the control of Sikhs. If racism makes them feel uneasy in a country like Britain, those of them who can leave because they possess the skills that all countries need. Some will go to the emerging opportunities provided in the Pacific region. Britain could be left to poor whites and others who lack the ability to get up and go. One thing is certain: Sikhs will continue to use their energies, based on their philosophy of honest hard work, to advance themselves and the societies in which they settle. Whether more of them will leave India depends upon a resolution of the Punjab crisis and national stability as well as opportunities afforded abroad. One thing seems certain, the kind of mass migration, which resulted in about 150,000 Sikhs moving to Britain, is unlikely to be repeated anywhere.

Some disapora Sikhs have a vision of completing the Gurus' work by taking their message to countries that they were not able to visit themselves. They see the purpose of migration not only in terms of self-fulfilment, but telling others about their religion. Sikhism, as has already been stated, is not a missionary religion, but Sikhs do regard Guru Nanak as a world teacher. This was the significance of the extensive journeys described in the Janam Sakhis. They also take seriously the words at the end of the congregational prayer, Ardas, 'Through Nanak may the glory of your Name increase and may the whole world be blessed by your grace'.

One way of doing this is by making the scriptures available to non-Sikhs in their own languages. Jarnail Singh, a migrant now settled in Canada, has completed a French translation. There are several English translations but mostly the language is archaic, based on the Authorised Version of the Bible, or unhelpful because the attempt to translate poetry into poetry is scarcely ever satisfactory. There are young Sikh scholars working in universities in the dispersion who wish to produce a modern English translation that will help Westerners to understand Sikhism **and** provide something which will be essential for Sikhs growing up in English-speaking countries in the twenty-first century, if they are to be able to identify with, and be nourished by, their parental spirituality.

Modern issues such as those mentioned in the chapter on ethics will be addressed by Sikhs outside India primarily.

Just as Christianity is often captive to European culture, so Sikhism is restricted by its Punjabi ties. If Sikhism is to sever its links with Punjabi culture, it is the Sikhs beyond India who will enable it to do this. Those within Punjab may see no problem, in the same way that it is black Christians who have had to open

figure 17 young Sikhs in Delhi growing up within their tradition. Nagar kirtan on the birthday of Guru Gobind Singh

the eyes of white Christians to their possible distortion of the Gospel. This said, however, the base of Sikhism in the foreseeable future, and perhaps for all time, will be Punjab.

In 2003 the most expensive gurdwara in the world was opened in Southall, England. The cost is estimated at £13,000,000 but a figure of £24,000,000 has also been mentioned. The 1951 census gave only 330 members of the population as being born in new commonwealth countries. Ten years later this had risen to 2540. In 2001 the number of Sikhs in Ealing is 25,625, of which Southall is a part, and in neighbouring Hounslow 18,265. (2001 is the first census since 1851 where a question on religious adherence has been asked.) Sikhs first met in a hall, hired on Sundays, for Diwan, a copy of the Guru Granth Sahib being taken from a private house. Some 40 or 50 people attended the gathering for worship. In 1961 a house was purchased, two rooms were converted for use as a gurdwara. In 1967 a dairy was bought which, in 1975 was expanded when the next door building was obtained. Ten years later the land on which the new gurdwara now stands, was bought in Park Avenue but the foundation stone was not laid until 1999. The purpose-built gurdwara is centrally heated, has an underground car park and another for handicapped persons. These are taken by lift to the main hall. Special attention has been given to their needs, possibly for the first time in the history of gurdwara construction. The langar hall accommodates 2000 people. There are also rooms for wedding receptions and for use as classrooms to meet the needs of extensive educational programmes. The palki sahib, weighing 1000 kg, was constructed in India and shipped to England.

The story of this new gurdwara is an expression of the maturation and confidence of Sikhs in one particular part of the diaspora. It can be mirrored in many other countries.

Sikh population

The number of Sikhs worldwide can only be estimated. Several websites provide information but figures vary widely from about 23 million to 39 million. Much depends on the method of computation used. The total Indian population in 2001 is given as 1,027,015,247. Religious statistics are yet to be provided. Two per cent is a popular proportion given to Sikhs, hence about 23 million. It is obvious that Sikhs are to be found in greater numbers in some areas than others, for example, Punjab, Haryana and Delhi. If Punjab has 24,289,296 and 25 per cent are Sikhs, that will give them a total of 6,072,324 in the state. If Delhi's population is 13,782,976, and 10 per cent are Sikhs, that will give a further 1,378,297. Whether the estimates of 25 per cent and 10 per cent respectively for Punjab and Delhi are accurate will not be known for some years. Meanwhile estimates should be treated with caution, bearing in mind that all groups are more inclined to favour higher estimates than depress their numbers.

In the countries of the diaspora there is similar uncertainty, especially regarding the USA. Some estimates give 1 million for the whole of North America, others for the United States alone. More reliable is the census total of 2001 for Canada, 147,000; for Australia, 12,000 in 1996; for New Zealand 2800 in 2001; and for the UK, 336,000. Malaysia has about 57,000 and Singapore 20,000. Latin America is said to have 9000 and Europe, excluding the UK, a further 130,000, which seems overlarge. African numbers are very uncertain. We are left with the inclination to accept 23 million as the total of Sikhs worldwide.

What can be stated with certainty is that Sikhs have emigrated principally to the English-speaking countries and those that were formerly part of the British Empire, for reasons to do with culture and language.

taking it further

Further reading

The Heritage of the Sikhs Harbans Singh; Monohar, India, 1985. A comprehensive and clear survey of Sikh history written by one of Sikhism's most eminent scholars.

The B40 Janam Sakhi Translated WH McLeod; Guru Nanak University, Amritsar, 1980. The most convenient translation of a Janam Sakhi into English.

Sikh Shrines in India GS Randhir: Ministry of Information, India, 1990. A list of gurdwaras for any traveller going to India. Most guide books seem to miss out Sikh shrines.

A Popular Dictionary of Sikhism W Owen Cole and Piara Singh Sambhi, Curzon Press, 1990. An extension of the glossary for anyone needing more detail.

Sikhism and Christianity W Owen Cole and Piara Singh Sambhi, Macmillan, 1993. Some readers may be interested in interfaith dialogue. This is the book for them.

Textual Sources for the Study of Sikhism Edited and translated by WH McLeod, Chicago University, 1990. The best available collection of the main Sikh writings.

Hymns from Bhai Gurdas Gobind Singh Mansukhani. Sikh Missionary Society, 10, Featherstone Road, Southall, London, UB2 5AA, 1988. Many pamphlets on various aspects of Sikhism can be obtained from this source.

The Name of my Beloved Nikky Guninder Kaur Singh, HarperCollins, 1996. A modern translation of the major hymns regularly used in congregational worship and personal devotion.

The Wisdom of Sikhism Charanjit K AjitSingh, One World Books, 2001. An attractively illustrated and presented compilation.

The Guru Granth Sahib, Pashaura Singh, Oxford, 2000.

The Bhagats of the Guru Granth Sahib, Pashaura Singh, Oxford, 2003.

The Making of Sikh Scripture, Gurinder Singh Mann, Oxford, 2001.

Garland Around my Neck Patwant Singh and Harinder Kaur Sekhon, DTF Publishers and Distributors, Birmingham, England, 2001. A fascinating account of the life and work of a famous twentieth-century exemplar of seva.

Sikhism Hew McLeod, Penguin, 1997. An excellent survey by one of the world's leading scholars.

The Arts of the Sikh Kingdoms Susan Stronge, editor, Victoria and Albert Museum, 1999. The book of the Khalsa tercentenary exhibition. A fine study of an important period of Sikh art and history.

The Sikhs: Their Religious Beliefs and Practices W Owen Cole and Piara Singh Sambhi, Sussex Academic Press, 1995. A comprehensive account; used by many university departments worldwide.

The Golden Temple Patwant Singh, ET Publishing Ltd., Hong Kong, 1988. The coffee table appearance should not deter anyone from reading this important exploration of the most famous Sikh gurdwara.

Anandpur; City of Bliss Mohinder Singh

The Golden Temple Mohinder Singh

Maharaja Ranjit Singh Mohinder Singh and Rishi Singh

Pilgrimage to Hemkunt: Jaswant Singh Neki

These are the first of a series of lavishly illustrated, informative books written by leading Sikh scholars. Published by UBS Publishers' Distributors Ltd. and the National Institute of Panjab Studies, Bhai Vir Singh Marg, New Delhi, 110 001.

Most of the Indian publications should be available from Susan Gole, Jaya books, 14 Oakford Road, London, NW5 1AH; 020 7267 4346 but visits should be made by appointment.

Sikhism on the Internet

The author acknowledges the help of Joy Barrow in assembling this section.

www.sikhnet.com

www.sikhe.com

www.sikhspirit.com

www.keertan.org

Websites come and go with considerable rapidity. Readers are advised to undertake their own searches.

Adi   first in the sense of primary, original

Akal Purukh   the Being beyond time; God

Akhand path   continuous, uninterrupted reading of the Guru Granth Sahib

Amrit   nectar; mixture of sugar and water used at initiation

Amrit pahul   Sikh initiation ceremony

Amritdhari   one who has been initiated

Amritpan karna   another term for the initiation ceremony

Ardas   the Sikh prayer

Atman   soul, self

Avatar   'descent' or incarnation of a deity, usually a form of Vishnu

Baba   title given to a respected (often elderly) man

Bani   word, or speech; the material contained in the Guru Granth Sahib

Baoli   a well, with steps down to the water level

Bhai Sahib   phrase often used to address or refer to a granthi

Bhog   concluding ceremony of a Path

Bhangra   form of dance traditionally performed by men

Brahma vidya   knowledge of brahman

Brahmacharya   student; first stage of life in Indian tradition

Brahmgiani   one who has knowledge of brahman; an enlightened person

Brahman   Hindu name for the impersonal supreme Reality

Brahmin   purist Hindu varna from whom priests are drawn

Chamar leather worker, so impure as to be outside Hindu caste system

Chanani canopy over Guru Granth Sahib

Chauri fan waved over Guru Granth Sahib to show respect for it

Chuhra member of sweeper class so impure as to be outside Hindu caste system

Darbar Sahib the name of the complex of buildings in Amritsar popularly known as the Golden Temple

Darshan grace giving glance or sight of a guru or Guru Granth Sahib

Dasam Granth compilation of writings attributed to the tenth Guru

Dehra settlement of a spiritual teacher where his followers gather

Dharamsala early name for a gurdwara, now often a hostel for pilgrims

Diwan Sikh act of public worship

Diwan hall room in a gurdwara where diwan takes place

Dohli departure ceremony at the end of a wedding

Gaddi a guru's seat of authority

Gayatri mantra most sacred Hindu scriptural verse

Giani a person learned in Sikh teachings

Gidda form of dance traditionally performed by women

Gora white; used of Western Sikh converts

Got exogamous within a zat group

Granthi reader of the Sikh scriptures during services

Grihasthi (Punjabi) householder, second stage of life in Indian tradition

Gurdwara Sikh gathering for public worship

Gurmat Sikh teachings

Gurmatta decision based on Sikh teachings

Gurmukh one whose life is inspired by the Guru's teachings

Gurpurb anniversary of a Guru's birth or death

Guru Granth Sahib the Sikh scripture

Gutka a small book containing the chief hymns used in Sikh devotions

Halwa a pudding

Hari name of a Hindu god

Harimandir Sahib the gurdwara in the centre of the pool at Amritsar, popularly known by Westerners as the Golden Temple

Haumai self-centredness; a major vice in Sikh teaching

Hola Mohalla a Sikh festival

Hukam order; divine command

Hukam nama a decree issued by the Sikh community

Ik Oankar Sikh symbol for the oneness of God

izzat pride

Janam Sakhi collection of stories about one of the Gurus

Japji important hymn composed by Guru Nanak

Jatha army, group of touring musicians

Jathedar military leader

Jat Punjabi farmer zat

Jati endogamous caste group

Jivan mukt state of spiritual liberation while in the present body

Jot light; the divine spirit inside a person

Jura top knot

Kaccha underpants or trousers which are one of 5 Ks

Kal yug the fourth and present corrupt age according to Hindu teaching

Kala panni the black ocean which Hindus consider polluting to cross

Kalima Muslim statement of belief that God is one and Muhammad (peace be upon him) is his prophet

Kam pleasure, lust

Kangha comb; one of 5 Ks

Kara iron wristlet

Karah Parshad food which Sikhs share when they attend a gurdwara

Karma work; action; the consequences of action influencing rebirth

Karta Purukh a Sikh name for God, Creator

Katha lecture or sermon given in a gurdwara

Kaur literally princess, name taken by initiated Sikh women but used by many others

Kesh uncut hair (including a man's beard)

Keshdari Sikh who keeps the hair uncut

Keshki covering often worn between hair and turban or, by children, instead of turban, see also pattka

Khalsa community of initiated Sikh women and men

Khand stage on the path to liberation

Khanda Sikh symbol, double-edged sword

Khande da amrit initiation

Khatri merchantile caste to which the Gurus belonged

Khuda a Muslim name for God

Kirpan sword or sheath knife, one of 5 Ks, never called a dagger

Krodh anger, one of 5 evils

Kshatriya second Hindu varna; the warrior class

Kurahts vow made on initiation, breaking of which requires reinitiation

Langar meal served in gurdwara and/or place where it is served

Lavan marriage hymn

Lobh covetousness; one of 5 evils

Logos Greek philosophical term; the creative word

Man mukh self reliant

Mandir Hindu temple

Man mind, heart, soul

Manji sahib stool on which Guru Granth Sahib is placed

Masands administrators first appointed by Guru Amar Das

Muttha tekna bowing before a person, Guru Granth Sahib, or Nishan Sahib

Maya delusion of regarding worldly goals as real and permanent

Mela fair; occasion of some Sikh festivals

Milni the meeting of two families before a wedding

Miri temporal power

Moh attachment; one of 5 evils

Mona clean shaven Sikh with short hair (abusive, not to be used)

Mukti spiritual liberation

Mul Mantra a short verse encapsulating the essence of Sikh teaching

Mullah Muslim religious teacher

Murti representation of deity found in Hindu temples and homes

Nagar kirtan open air procession carrying Guru Granth Sahib

Nam simran meditation using hymns of the Gurus

Namdhari follower of the C19 Sikh reformers, Baba Balak Singh and Baba Ram Singh

Nanak Panthis devotees of Guru Nanak as distinct, often from Khalsa principles

Nihangs warriors who defended gurdwaras in past time (they live in encampments rather than houses)

Nirguna without physical form; used of God

Nirankar the Formless One; a name of God

Nirankari follower of C19th Sikh reformer Baba Dayal Singh

Nishan sahib flag flown from gurdwara

Pagri punjabi word for turban, also known as dastar

Panth the Sikh community worldwide

Panj kakkar the 5 Ks worn by initiated Sikh men and women

Parkash karna daily installation of the Guru Granth Sahib

Parmeshur/Parameshwara the Supreme Being, God

Patit a lapsed Khalsa Sikh

Pattka head covering often worn by sportsmen

Pir Muslim holy man

Piri spiritual power

Pothi book usually containing hymns of the Gurus

Qazi Muslim legal authority

Radhasoami Indian group founded in C19 strong in Punjab and with a modern international membership

Rag musical form

Ragi musician (who usually plays in gurdwara)

Rahit Maryada Khalsa code of discipline covering religious rites and ethical observances

Rahit Nama manual of conduct

Rama name of a popular Hindu deity

Ramgharia a distinctively Sikh zat of members of artisan castes, named after Jassa Singh a C18th military commander

Rig Veda the main Hindu scripture

Sadhu Hindu holy man

Saguna having physical form; used of God

Sahajdhari Sikh who does not keep the uncut hair or wear the turban

Samsara rebirth of the soul into another body until liberation is attained

Sangat local Sikh community; gurdwara congregation

Sangatia overseer of one of 22 groups into which Guru Amar Das divided the Panth; servant of the community

Sannyasin a man who has entered fourth stage of Hindu life

Sant Sikh holy man

Sant sipahi saint-soldier; what a Khalsa member should be

Saropa honour given by Panth or sangat

Sat Sri Akal usual Sikh greeting; 'Truth is Eternal'

Sati immolation of wife on husband's funeral pyre (illegal, always opposed by Sikhs, and by many Hindus)

Seva service voluntarily rendered

Shudra lowest of four Hindu varnas or classes; servant

Sidharan path non-continuous or interrupted reading of Guru Granth Sahib

Sufi Muslim mystic

Sukhasan laying to rest of Guru Granth Sahib

Sukhmani Sahib pearl of peace, famous hymn of Guru Arjan's

Swayya a poetic form found in the Guru Granth Sahib and Dasam Granth

Takht one of five Sikh seats of authority

Tankah breach of Khalsa discipline not requiring reinitiation, a kind of punishment involving community service

Tera 13, also 'yours'

Upanishad Hindu scripture based on discourse of a guru with his disciple

Vahiguru 'Wonderful One'; popular Sikh way of addressing God

Vaisakhi Sikh festival coinciding with new year

Vaishya third Hindu varna, merchant class

Vak advice received by randomly opening the Guru Granth Sahib

Vanaprastha third stage of Hindu life, semi-recluse

Varna class division of Hindu society

Var epic poem

Veda principal Hindu scripture

Vishvakarman Hindu god of craftsmen

Zat punjabi form of 'jati'; occupational caste group

index

teach® yourself

the A-Z of teach yourself

Hinduism
History, 101 Key Ideas
How to Win at Horse Racing
How to Win at Poker
HTML Publishing on the WWW
Human Anatomy & Physiology
Hungarian
Icelandic
Indian Head Massage
Indonesian
Information Technology, 101 Key Ideas
Internet, The
Irish
Islam
Italian
Italian, Beginner's
Italian Grammar
Italian Grammar, Quick Fix
Italian, Instant
Italian, Improve your
Italian Language, Life & Culture
Italian Verbs
Italian Vocabulary
Japanese
Japanese, Beginner's
Japanese, Instant
Japanese Language, Life & Culture
Japanese Script, Beginner's
Java
Jewellery Making
Judaism
Korean
Latin
Latin American Spanish
Latin, Beginner's
Latin Dictionary
Latin Grammar
Letter Writing Skills
Linguistics
Linguistics, 101 Key Ideas
Literature, 101 Key Ideas
Mahjong
Managing Stress
Marketing
Massage
Mathematics
Mathematics, Basic
Media Studies
Meditation
Mosaics
Music Theory
Needlecraft
Negotiating
Nepali

Norwegian
Origami
Panjabi
Persian, Modern
Philosophy
Philosophy of Mind
Philosophy of Religion
Philosophy of Science
Philosophy, 101 Key Ideas
Photography
Photoshop
Physics
Piano
Planets
Planning Your Wedding
Polish
Politics
Portuguese
Portuguese, Beginner's
Portuguese Grammar
Portuguese, Instant
Portuguese Language, Life & Culture
Postmodernism
Pottery
Powerpoint 2002
Presenting for Professionals
Project Management
Psychology
Psychology, 101 Key Ideas
Psychology, Applied
Quark Xpress
Quilting
Recruitment
Reflexology
Reiki
Relaxation
Retaining Staff
Romanian
Russian
Russian, Beginner's
Russian Grammar
Russian, Instant
Russian Language, Life & Culture
Russian Script, Beginner's
Sanskrit
Screenwriting
Serbian
Setting up a Small Business
Shorthand, Pitman 2000
Sikhism
Spanish
Spanish, Beginner's
Spanish Grammar
Spanish Grammar, Quick Fix

Spanish, Instant
Spanish, Improve your
Spanish Language, Life & Culture
Spanish Starter Kit
Spanish Verbs
Spanish Vocabulary
Speaking on Special Occasions
Speed Reading
Statistical Research
Statistics
Swahili
Swahili Dictionary
Swedish
Tagalog
Tai Chi
Tantric Sex
Teaching English as a Foreign Language
Teaching English One to One
Teams and Team-Working
Thai
Time Management
Tracing your Family History
Travel Writing
Trigonometry
Turkish
Turkish, Beginner's
Typing
Ukrainian
Urdu
Urdu Script, Beginner's
Vietnamese
Volcanoes
Watercolour Painting
Weight Control through Diet and
  Exercise
Welsh
Welsh Dictionary
Welsh Language, Life & Culture
Wills and Probate
Wine Tasting
Winning at Job Interviews
Word 2002
World Faiths
Writing a Novel
Writing for Children
Writing Poetry
Xhosa
Yoga
Zen
Zulu

available from bookshops and on-line retailers